PITARA

A MEDLEY OF MEMORIES, MUSINGS, MISCHIEF, AND MEANING.

RAJAN NARAYAN

__For Udbhav__
Whose arrival turned noise into story,
sleepless nights into characters,
and this once-wandering mind into a writer's home.

You were my first audience.
You laughed at the nonsense,
listened to the silences,
and unknowingly opened the lid of this Pitara.

Everything here began with you.

Contents

Contents

Preface

This book isn't a grand declaration. It's a rummaging —
through memory, moments, mischief, and meaning.

It holds no pretence of profundity. Some stories here
might make you laugh out loud, others might sneak up
behind you and whisper something you didn't expect.
Many are anchored in childhood, some in everyday
adulthood, and a few in that peculiar no-man's-land where
memory and reflection blur.

These pieces were never originally written with the
idea of a book in mind. They were simply written — often
in a burst, sometimes late at night, usually unplanned. They
come from the same place where old songs live, where
smells from your grandmother's kitchen hide, and where
that one street in your hometown still looks exactly like you
remember it.

If there's a thread that binds them, it's this: **I wrote
these because I had to.** Because something in me
remembered, or laughed, or hurt, or noticed — and wanted
to say it aloud.

Pitara means a treasure chest, a box of bits and bobs,
of keepsakes and curios. That's what this is. I hope you
find something inside that feels familiar. Or better still,
something that makes you want to open your own pitara
and see what's been sitting there all these years.

Acknowledgements

This book wouldn't have happened without a whole tribe behind it.

To **Geeta**—my wife, my occasional co-conspirator, and my fiercest believer—thank you for gently but firmly nudging me to write, even when I wasn't sure I had anything to say. You didn't just believe in the writer in me—you insisted he show up.

To my sister **Renuka**—your quiet wisdom, relentless encouragement, and sharp editorial eye have been my anchor through many drafts and doubts. You've been part editor, part cheerleader, part compass.

To **my parents**—thank you for raising us in a home filled with books, conversation, curiosity, and debate. Around that dining table, a writer took shape, whether he knew it or not.

To my **cousins and extended family**—thank you for the stories, the laughter, the leg-pulls, and the memories. This book carries echoes of you all.

To my **friends and ex-colleagues**—thank you for reading, reflecting, questioning, and cheering me on. Some of you didn't even realise you were doing it—but you kept me going.

And a special thanks to young **Janvi Somnath Limble**—just 16, and a budding architect—for the brilliant cover illustration. You captured the spirit of Pitara with colour, imagination, and joy.

This **Pitara** may carry my name, but its contents belong to many lives, many voices, and a whole lot of love.

Thank you.

PART 1

CHAPTER ONE

DADDY COOL

When I first found out I was going to be a father, a wave of emotions swept through me. But amidst all that, one question kept rising to the surface:

What would be the one thing that defines my relationship with my child?

Days passed without an answer. Then one night, returning home wearily from yet another late shift, I ate a lonely dinner and quietly lay down next to my sleeping wife. I placed my hand on her pregnant stomach — and it hit me.

I'd probably never have the kind of time I wanted with my child. On most days, an hour if I was lucky. That night, I made a promise to myself:

Our bond would be built on laughter.

Not discipline, not tradition, not grand lessons. Just pure, unfiltered joy.

I've never considered myself particularly bright, but I do have one weapon — I can spin a yarn. Questionable quality, but hey, I use what I've got. From that night on, I began making up stories for my unborn child.

Silly, ridiculous ones. And I'd act them out in the dead of the night, while the world slept.

It was working. One night, my wife — half-asleep — asked me to stop.

"The baby's kicking. I can't sleep."

A few months later, our little UD arrived.

As per tradition, my wife moved in with her grandmother for a while. Every evening after work, I'd head over to see them. And while the rest of the house was busy, I'd lift my baby and tell him a new story. Each day. No repeats.

He listened with wide, unblinking eyes.
Sometimes, the family caught me mid-performance. Judging by their expressions, they thought I'd lost it.

Then one evening, an explosive laugh burst from that tiny body at one of my stupid tales.

From that day, every evening when I showed up at the door, he'd tear at his sheets, gurgling, eyes twinkling, arms outstretched. That recognition, that happiness — I don't think anything in the world can match it.

So began our nightly ritual. Story after story. For thirteen years.

We've built an entire universe —
Singsong and Billabong, the bird-and-squirrel duo.
Cheeku-Meeku-Tukku-Pukku, the monkeys. Their arch enemies: **Sunny-Bunny-Tinku-Minku**, the bunnies.
Udu the Space Ranger.
Kalia and Goria, inspired by our watchmen and lazier-than-thou watchdogs.
Caleo, the cat with a lion's attitude.
Kaalua, the shaggy dog with swag.

The stories are nonsense. Wild, absurd, and proudly pointless.
A milk-giving bull.
The Dark Lord doing the African samba.

A cat and dog winning the World Cup.

A gorilla getting a tooth pulled by unsuspecting dentists.

Anything goes — as long as it gets that laugh.

And what a laugh it is.

From his toothless baby giggles, to full-bodied, rolling-on-the-floor tear-streaming cackles. That laugh is my medal.

My son has always been a kind, patient, and generous audience. On the good days, he wipes his eyes and says, "Dad, today's was epic!"

Even when the stories bomb, he laughs and says, "Thanks, Dad."

There was a phase when I was told to be more 'father-like.' Stricter. More rules.

We tried. For a few months.

They were the worst months of my life.

He changed. That sparkle dimmed. He looked at me like he was searching for his dad in the face of this stranger.

I hated who I had become. I had let go of the most magical part of our bond.

Thankfully, sanity — and laughter — returned. And so did we.

One of my proudest moments?

At school, his class was once asked what their dads did.

He said, with full confidence and a smile:

"My dad's a joker."

He turns thirteen soon.

Sometimes I wonder — is it time to stop these stories?

But if stopping means losing that booming laugh, that shining face, that joy...

Then no, I'll never stop.

I'll probably be telling him stories on his wedding day.

And when he cradles his own baby, I'll still be at it.

Because that laughter?
    That laughter is everything.

CHAPTER TWO

LOVE IN THE TIMES OF INFLUENCERS

Mumbai, the city of dreams, where the air is thick with the scent of spice and ambition, had always been my playground. I am Shanayra, the spunky food blogger who critiques the newest, hippest joints with a sharp tongue and an eye for the perfect Instagram shot. My followers love me for my flair, my feistiness; they savor every word of my reviews like the dishes I write about. But recently, something had shifted. The comments under my posts, once filled with praise and heart-eyed emojis, were now littered with criticism.

"They're just glossy photos, no substance," they said. "She doesn't care about the food, just the fame."

It stung. It stung more than I would ever admit. I was at the top of my game, or so I thought, until he came along.

Vittal. I didn't know his name at first, only his work. His reviews were unlike anything I had seen before—raw, unpolished, but bursting with authenticity. While I was busy exploring the glitzy restaurants of South Bombay, Vittal was uncovering the hidden gems of the city—the tiny home-kitchens in crowded chawls, the street vendors who fed the working class, the little-known eateries that had been passed down through generations. His posts weren't like mine; they were just audio clips broadcasted on a local FM radio station, but they had a certain magic to them, a sincerity that resonated with people.

Curiosity got the better of me. Who was this person, this faceless food critic who was quickly gaining a reputation I had worked years to build? I was envious, yes, but more than that, I needed to know. I needed to understand how he was doing it. And that's when I found out the truth—Vittal was blind.

He was the son of a dabbawalla, one of the thousands of men who crisscross the city every day, delivering homemade meals from the kitchens of Mumbai's middle class to offices across the city. Vittal had grown up navigating the labyrinthine streets of the city with his father, his world defined by sounds, smells, and the feel of the air as it changed from one neighborhood to another. His blindness, which had taken his sight as a child, had only sharpened his other senses, and it was these that he relied on to judge the food he tasted.

I had to meet him. More than that, I had to know his secret.

When I first approached Vittal, he was wary. He had no interest in fame or followers, and he certainly didn't want anything to do with someone like me—someone he saw as superficial, chasing likes and comments rather than the real essence of food. But I persisted, and slowly, he began to let me into his world. We traveled together through the narrow lanes of Dharavi, where the smell of freshly fried samosas mingled with the acrid scent of industrial waste. We visited tiny kitchens where the cooks, mostly women, stirred large pots over open flames, their faces lined with years of hard work and struggle. Vittal would take in the scent of the spices, feel the texture of the food, and then taste it, his expression always one of deep concentration.

"This," he would say, "this is food made with love. You can taste the passion in every bite."

It was something I had never considered before, the idea that food could convey emotion, that it could tell a story of struggle, of survival, of pride. And Vittal was right. These were not the polished, Instagram-worthy dishes I was used to, but they were real, and they were good.

As I spent more time with Vittal, I began to see the city through his eyes—or rather, through his other senses. Mumbai, with all its chaos and contradictions, became a place of endless discovery. The clanging of the local trains, the incessant honking of taxis, the chatter of street vendors, all became part of a symphony that Vittal navigated with ease. He knew the city better than anyone I had ever met, not through sight, but through touch, smell, and sound. And the food—oh, the food. It was as if he could taste the soul of Mumbai in every dish, and he taught me to do the same.

It was around this time that I signed a deal with a production house and an OTT channel. I knew Vittal's story was one that needed to be told, and I wanted to be the one to tell it. I wanted to show the world what I had seen, what I had learned from him. The series of videos we made together went viral almost immediately. People were captivated by this blind food critic who could describe the taste of a dish with such vivid detail, even though he had never seen it. Vittal became a sensation, and I... well, I basked in the glow of our success.

But as the fame grew, so did the pressure. Vittal, who had never wanted any of this, began to retreat. The spotlight was too bright, the attention too overwhelming. He was a simple man, content with his life in the slums of Mumbai, helping his father deliver tiffins and discovering hidden culinary treasures. But now, he was being pulled into a world he didn't understand and didn't want to be a part of.

I was too caught up in the whirlwind of success to notice what was happening to him. I was doing interviews, signing deals, and planning our next series. Vittal, meanwhile, was disappearing, slipping further and further away from me. Until one day, he was gone.

No one knew where he had gone, not even his father. The videos stopped, the buzz faded, and soon, Vittal was just a memory, a brief sensation that had come and gone like so many others in this city. I moved on—or at least I tried to. But something kept nagging at me, a sense of unfinished business, of something left unsaid.

Then one day, months after Vittal had disappeared, I ran into his father. It was by chance, on the street near my office. He was delivering a tiffin, just like he had done every day for years. I stopped him, asked him if he had heard from Vittal. The look on his face told me everything.

"He's gone," his father said simply. "He slipped from the train one morning while we were working. He didn't survive."

The words hit me like a punch to the gut. I had lost touch with Vittal, lost sight of what really mattered, and now he was gone. But his father handed me a small tape recorder, the kind you could pick up at any roadside stall in the city. "He left this for you," he said before walking away.

That night, I sat alone in my apartment, the city's noise muted by the thick walls and the distance from the street below. I pressed play on the recorder, and Vittal's voice filled the room.

"Shanayra," he began, his voice steady but filled with a quiet emotion I had never heard from him before. "I don't know if you'll ever hear this, but if you do, I want you to know something. I've never seen the world, but I've tasted it, felt it, smelled it. I've known it in ways that others don't. And I've known you. You're like the city, full of life, full of dreams, but you're also full of noise. You need to listen more, feel more. There's a whole world out there, and it's not all about the glitz and the glamour. It's about the people, the stories, the food made with love. That's what I wanted to share with you, with everyone. But maybe I didn't do it the right way. Maybe I should have stayed in the shadows. I don't know. All I know is that I cared for you, more than I ever let on. And I hope, in some way, you cared for me too."

The recording ended, and I sat there, tears streaming down my face. Vittal had given me so much, and I had taken it all without thinking about what it might cost him. I had lost him, and now, all I had left was his voice, his words, and the lessons he had taught me.

The next morning, I made a decision. I went to the FM station where Vittal had first started his journey, and I asked to take over his slot. I wanted to continue what he had begun, to honor his memory and the passion he had for food and for the people who made it. But I didn't want to do it in the way I had before, with flashy videos and Instagram posts. I wanted to do it his way, through sound, through storytelling, through the radio.

And so, that's what I did. Every week, I would go on air and share a new story, a new discovery, just as Vittal had. I visited the same tiny kitchens, met the same people, and tasted the same food, but this time, I did it with a new understanding, a new appreciation. I learned to taste with my heart, to listen with my soul, and to see the world in a way I never had before.

Mumbai is still the same city it always was—noisy, chaotic, full of contradictions. But for me, it's different now. It's a place where I found something real, something true, something that goes beyond the surface. And as I share these stories with the people of this city, I hope that they, too, can find a little bit of what I found with Vittal—a taste of something genuine, something made with love.

Vittal is gone, but his legacy lives on, in every story I tell, in every dish I taste, in every person I meet. And in that way, he's still here, still a part of this city, still a part of me.

CHAPTER THREE

NO MEDALS, HIGH SPIRITS: THE INDIAN PSYCHE

There's a famous Nike ad that says, *"You don't win the silver. You lose the gold."*

As the Rio Olympics drew to a close, India stood on the brink of finishing without a single medal in its kitty. Strangely, this didn't seem to dampen the spirits of the nation. Most Indians simply took the loss in their stride—and, in true Indian style, went on to celebrate the very athletes who *lost*.

The folks at Nike and their ad agency must be scratching their heads. What did they miss? Where did they go wrong in understanding India?

While American, Australian, Chinese, German—even Fijian—athletes wept over the loss of a gold medal, we Indians were busy clapping for effort. For us, *"We participated and did our best. It's fine if we didn't win,"* seems a perfectly acceptable response.

I'm not here to judge whether that's right or wrong. But it did get me wondering—why do we Indians seem to have such a different attitude towards winning and losing than most other countries?

Perhaps the answer lies in our very philosophy of existence.

In the West, life is seen as linear. You only live once. Therefore, you must make the most of it. The ultimate goal is a kind of immortality—achieved through records, medals, achievements that live on after you. It's no surprise then, that Western civilizations have meticulously recorded, rewarded, and celebrated victory and performance for centuries.

But Indian philosophy views life as **circular**.

We believe we're trapped in a cycle of birth and rebirth—*samsara*. No matter what you do, you'll be back here again to continue your journey. Only those who transcend material desires can break free from this endless loop and attain liberation—*moksha*.

So what's the big deal about an Olympic record or a gold medal?

It's not the end of the world.

There will be many more Olympics. Countless, infinite editions in the lifetime of this ever-expanding universe. And in that infinitude, there will be endless chances to win. So why fret over this one?

After all, we're all just energy—constantly transforming, bound to this universe that itself expands, contracts, and explodes into life again in a never-ending cycle. Neither you nor I—neither Dipa Karmakar nor Michael Phelps—can escape that cosmic rhythm.

Eventually, we'll all catch up.

For now, let's celebrate. Not winning. Not losing. But being.

Jai Hind.

CHAPTER FOUR

THIRD-GRADE STORYTELLER

The first yarn I ever spun was to save myself from being torn apart by the sharp talons of Ms. Lucy Furtado, my class teacher in the 3rd grade of school. Lucy was young and pretty but short-tempered. Who wouldn't be, having to manage 60 unruly kids, never seeming to fear punishment? But Lucy had developed her own mechanism of unruly kid control: she had grown her nails long till they resembled the talons of the fiercest birds of prey. With these, she dug into the soft arms and cheeks of any child unlucky enough to get on her wrong side, till he or she howled in pain—never daring after that harrowing experience to misbehave for the rest of the year.

Having recently been at the receiving end of those blood-red claws, I was petrified of repeating the painful experience. Unfortunately, one day I had forgotten to complete my homework and realized I was due for a bird-hit. A child in need is creative indeed. My mind leapt from reason to reason even as she raised her claws to strike me! Closer and closer they came, so close that I could smell the chalk-dust on them.

"Wait miss, we had a flash visit from my uncle!" The talons paused for a fraction of a second before continuing their deadly journey towards my plump cheeks.

"That's hardly a reason," they snapped.

"But he's a war hero and had stopped over on a mission." I screamed in consternation.

Lucy looked over the talons. "War-hero uncle with a mission?"

That wasn't completely untrue. My uncle was indeed a war hero—he'd been a part of the Indian Army during WWII—but had long since retired. Still, I built a whole lot of imagination on that sliver of truth: he hadn't stopped by the previous evening, nor was he on a mission. And he was completely oblivious to the rescue act he was performing for his nephew at that very moment.

Thinking quickly, I made a few alterations to history, mixed it with some inspiration from Alistair MacLean, and a lot of my budding imagination to create a modified 'all-new fictitious uncle'.

Meet him! A major in the commando unit, he'd supposedly flown countless sorties during the '71 war, been captured several times, and imaginatively escaped each time—through wits, guts, and some borrowed one-liners—eventually leading our country to victory. His missions, like every fictitious hero's flights of fancy, continued well after the war, ensuring the peace of our nation.

Lucy was moved! Most importantly, young as I was, I had quickly recognized the misty, lovelorn look that crept into the eyes of young, single, and lonely Ms. Lucy. Craftily, I had recast my uncle—from the middle-aged married father-of-three that he was—into a young, dashing singleton yearning for feminine love.

The story was a super-duper hit with its audience of one! Soon, I was her favourite in class—getting a few extra marks in all subjects, and none from her talons.

One unfortunate day, after listening to the many sequels of his escapades, she evinced an interest in meeting my uncle. Cursing my overactive imagination under my breath, I somehow dodged the inevitable by citing the critical nature of his missions.

But midway through the year, when I felt her interest—and my marks—flagging, I realized I needed to give my stories a booster shot to reignite her enthusiasm.

As luck would have it, that very evening, my mother received a red handbag as a gift from my father. Not finding the bright red colour suitable to her taste, she asked my sisters if they wanted it. Imagine their collective shock when I jumped into the fray and fought tooth and nail for it! I resorted to everything a 7-year-old could do: tantrums, tears, rolling on the floor, emotional blackmail. Finally, disgusted and bewildered by my actions, they caved in and I emerged triumphant—with the red handbag in my, well, hand.

The next day, I reached school early and quietly handed the red leather bag to Lucy as a gift from my appreciative (and fictitious) uncle. The love-struck expression on her face as she accepted it remains etched in my mind to this day. She picked it up as though it was Romeo's gift to Juliet and lovingly placed it in her cupboard next to the table in our classroom.

Pangs of remorse hit me whenever, in between her tight and tough schedules, I caught sight of her admiring and caressing the bag.

The year finally came to a close. Class three was a success—but my travails were not over yet. My sternest test was reserved for results day, when, accompanied by my father and sisters, I returned to class to pick up my report card.

That day, I cringed and cowered in embarrassment as poor innocent Lucy waxed eloquently about my imaginary uncle to my befuddled father and dumbstruck sisters. She wasn't letting go of my report card—her body language seemed to plead with my father to let her meet his younger brother at least once.

My poor father stammered and stuttered in embarrassment and finally went completely silent in the face of Lucy's heartfelt entreaties.

And then it happened.

She rushed to the cupboard to pull out some papers—and out popped the bright, shiny red leather handbag! The look on my sisters' faces was a sight not for the faint-hearted. Silently, both turned to me, pure murder in their eyes! I cringed. My eyes pleaded with them, promising a lifetime of servitude, begging them to hold back their words.

We returned home in complete silence.

The next day, when the shock wore off, the entire family burst out laughing as I sheepishly blurted out the whole story... a story they continue to rag me about to this very day.

CHAPTER FIVE

RANISTHAN

In a land of kings aplenty
Were once four—high and mighty—
Who fought for land and title,
Always ready for a battle,
For reasons real... or imaginary.
    The country suffered most:
Drought.
Famine.
Egos.
    What kings they were,
But slaves in truth—
Flaunting Rolls and Vuitton,
Running on the blood of peasants.
    In the drunken haze of their orgy,
They heard of a princess—of great beauty.
Graceful.
Wealthy.
Unclaimed.
    As one, they arose—
Each claiming her for his own.
They raised their armies,
And fought.

Through summers, winters,
Round the clock,
Till no home remained untouched.
    The armies grew ragged.
Death haunted every hamlet.
But the royals? Unaffected.
Their pride? Unyielding.
    The girl was of finer steel.
She saw her country bleed.
And made an unthinkable choice.
She killed herself—
And changed the equation.
    A hundred years have passed.
But what have we learnt, alas?
Men still fight and die.
Women still burn alive.

CHAPTER SIX

HOW I ALMOST NEVER HAPPENED

Tile of film: *How I Almost Never Happened.*
Setting:*Delhi and Mumbai mid 60's*
<u>Summary of main characters:</u>
Dad:*Cool dude from Delhi. An officer in the Home Ministry, enjoying his (soon to be curtailed) independence. Living in Karol Baug by himself and mostly on parathas, lassi with exercise in the mornings and cycling to work like thousand other Delhiites. A secure, government job, great Punjabi food for lunch and dinner, one English, one Hindi and one Tamil movie every week viewed and discussed to death with Tamil and Punjabi friends. And of course, one classic piece of literature every month. In short, he was the 60's equivalent of a yuppie. But unknown to him, the stars had worked out an altogether different course for his future.*

Grandpa:*My mom's father, widower. Retired as a senior executive from a multinational company. Among the few Indians to graduate from college in the 1920's. Exceptional thinker, brilliant writer, strict disciplinarian, extremely short-tempered and temperamental. Imagine an educated, English-speaking (clipped tone!) lanky version of Amrish Puri in*

DDLJ!

Mom:*Terrified of her father. Will mostly sulk, cry and look confused during the movie.*

Film opens in Dadar, Bombay. The year is 1963. Grandpa is sitting facing his durbar. He smokes using a silver filter. Trembling in front of him are the sisters, brothers of his long-departed wife and their respective spouses. They are pleading with him to arrange the marriage of his last daughter, my mom who would soon turn 21. After dishing them an earful for doubting his earnestness in conducting his daughter's wedding, he carelessly throws a note at his brother-in-law and barks, "Take this and put an ad in the newspaper and report to me!" The entire crew vanish like Houdini's dove.

Cut to a few days later, Grandpa is viewing the bro-in-law with stern suspicion wondering why the man seemed pleased. "Anna, for just an additional Rs.2/- the newspaper agreed to release the ad in their Delhi edition too, so I took it."

"You blackguard!" thundered grandpa, "Delhi is a city of wastrels I say! Only Bombay it was to be. Now rush to the paper and get me back my Rs. 2/-." Too late, the ad had been published. The bro-in-law from then on was persona non grata at grandpa's home for good.

Applications from Bombay were received and reviewed. There were many, for mom was prettier than a princess. "What rubbish! BA third class, no way! Wants girl to look after elderly parents? My daughter is not a nurse! Transferable job? no way. Wants us to go to their house? NO!"

And for the few who managed to meet all parameters, failure was guaranteed in the interview! "English not good enough! Looks like a crow! How dare your family demand dowry! Poor in GK! hasn't read much beyond Earl Stanley Gardner pah! No scope for promotion in job! Dull as ditch-water! Hasn't heard of Marx or Mao! Fail, fail, fail!"

Things weren't looking good for poor mom and her concerned aunts and uncles were defeated in their attempts to convince my irascible grandpa.

But then, as luck would have it, the Rs. 2/- was about to pay dividends!

In Delhi, unknown to Dad, his over-enthusiastic stenographer, a fellow Tamilian, Jayaraman, was worried that my father was making no attempt to tie the knot and decided to take matters into his own hands. His eyes fell on the matrimonial ad that mom's hapless uncle had inadvertently placed in the Delhi edition of the paper. Now stenographers in Delhi are known for their pathetic command of the English language. Ask Pakistan's ISI if in doubt, because it takes them forever to decipher the notes typed by the English-challenged stenos of North/South blocks. But this steno was of a determined heart even if his English was cringe-worthy. Without wasting any time, he rolled in a paper in his trusted typewriter and dashed off a letter to grandpa, posing as Dad, seeking mom's alliance.

Grandpa was delighted to receive that letter, He laughed his heart out at the language and called all relatives home including the red-faced bro-in-law, to read out its pitiful contents with relish. Then he thumped his chest to underscore how the letter was testimony to his understanding of the philistines from Delhi and proceeded to declare that he would personally write a sarcastic retort to this barbarian who dared to seek his daughter's hand in marriage, noting that his wit and sarcasm may in reality be lost on the uncouth man.

Now the letter had my dad's Delhi residence address. So, one day, out of the blue, my dad's happy-going-lucky mood was interrupted by a sarcastic letter from a man who purported to having received dad's offer of marriage for his daughter. Dad being dad, soon unearthed the whole plot and confronted his well-meaning steno who accepted his guilt but mentioned it was done with a good intention behind it.

Not wanting to leave behind a bad impression, dad wrote back to grandpa explaining the whole thing in good humor and wondered if his language was good enough for grandpa to grant him an interview.

Grandpa was flummoxed. He was used to two kinds of people all through his life: One type were those who cowered at him in fright and the other type were those who fought with him and never spoke to him thereafter. Here on the other hand, was a young man who clearly had understood and accepted his sarcasm in good faith and replied, (he had to grudgingly accept) fittingly.

Mom's aunt at this point beseeched him to at least meet up with the man's relative. And so, grandpa agreed to first meet dad's sister and husband who lived in Bombay. Now this particular uncle of mine also happened to be of the temperamental sorts. There should have been fireworks during that first meeting but somehow on that one day the two men got on like a house on fire instead, and the marriage was fixed.

So, dad landed up on the day of his engagement and was promptly called by grandpa for a meeting. A grilling was in store for dad. Mom's uncles and her brothers-in-law tried to warn dad but grandpa just didn't give him any time. He told dad to report to his house as soon as he disembarked from the Delhi train. Grandpa was prowling like a caged tiger with a long list of questions in his hands. Without giving dad the permission to sit or see mom, he launched into dad with his multi-topic rapid-fire exam. Two hours later grandpa was in a state of shock. This young man had answered his every question correctly without letting his smile slip or letting go of the twinkle in his eyes!

He took a break. During which dad met mom. After that, if anything, dad's resolve only grew firmer. This was the girl he would marry, he told himself.

The engagement was conducted that evening. At the end of which the temperamental uncle made the cardinal mistake of requesting grandpa to buy dad a suit and a watch. Grandpa's right eyebrow went up several notches. "I suppose the boy doesn't read time till now? Does he ask people for the time?"

The temperamental uncle walked off in a huff and grandpa broke the engagement even before the ashes of the fire had cooled.

But dad to the rescue! He bought himself a watch, told the temperamental uncle that grandpa had come around and had purchased it, coaxed mom's terrified folks to convince grandpa that the boy was unaware of the watch request and in fact had never asked for one. After a few days of hectic negotiations, the marriage was back on track.

Moving fast, dad ensured the hall, priests, caterer and formalities were booked and ordered, by co-opting members of his own and mom's family in fixing the marriage, since grandpa had refused to take any effort in managing the event.

Finally, the day of the marriage dawned and by now even dad's patient smile was beginning to slip under all the effort. But somehow his luck held and the marriage took place on 28th August 1964.

At the end of the ceremony, the temperamental uncle made the mistake of reminding grandpa that he still had the duty of arranging for the couple's breakfast after their nuptials. Grandpa realizing that the marriage was done and for once, he couldn't threaten to call it off, removed a currency note from his shirt and flung it on the temperamental uncle asking him do the needful himself! It was the last flash-point for the day that dad managed to douse.

Dad and mom shifted to Bombay permanently in 1969 and I was born a year later. We would every fortnight, unfailingly visit grandpa who had come round to admitting that Dad had finally proven to be an agreeable son-in-law. In fact, they got on quite well as I recall and grandpa transferred some of the affection he had developed for dad, to me. For much to everyone's surprise, he'd allow me to sit on his knee and pull his long white beard while he would smile indulgently at me!

Dad remained close to him and always listened to him patiently. Even today he recalls his father-in-law with the warmest of sentiment. I guess that's the way it should be.

Tragedies can easily be converted into comedies if we take things in the right spirit.

I hope, dear friends that you agree with me!

Part 2

CHAPTER SEVEN

I'm Rich And Happy

I'm a *happy* man. Of course, there are times when I'm not so happy. Especially when Tukoo goes missing sometimes in the morning. But so far, the great Khodiya has been merciful and has watched over my Tukoo, like I would.

But then I am *happier* too. Those are the days when me and others gather together over mahua and meat. Very soon everyone's singing and swaying rhythmically to the beat. Then the great Lord *Biri* peeks from the end of the sky, reminding us of daily duties.

This is time of the day when I'm *happiest* because I'm deep within Mother *Abujhmaad*, looking for her gifts. Mother never disappoints us; she is kind and gives us all that our stomachs can hold.

I am *happiest* when I'm lying with my little Chona, in the cool waters of the stream or in the shade of *Bahuna*, the great big tree of my forest where all living creatures find shelter and rest.

One day a pardesi visited us. They talk too much and are always unhappy. This one lived with us, talked too much and too fast. We listened not wanting to offend him.

Despite our efforts, he would get angry. One day his anger boiled over. He removed some dry leaf-like thing from his attire and tried to hand it to us. He was shocked to see my Pihu use it to make a fire. He screamed and shouted, putting his hand into the fire to extract it. He was blabbering all kinds of words that sounded like, Ambanee, Billgae and MANEE. Especially that last word. He kept screaming it, till he lost his voice. Hugging it he fell to the ground and began rolling on it.

When he recovered, he was silent. He collected all the MANEE, put it in his sack. Mumbling and laughing alternatively, he left.

I think MANEE must be his God. She must be a very different God from ours.

CHAPTER EIGHT

The Temple Tortoise

(This is a fictional story based on an annual trip we used to make as a family)

My mother makes an annual pilgrimage to a small temple about 100 km away from this megalopolis of a city. It's been a family ritual ever since I was a boy. She would rise early, painstakingly preparing a number of *koikattais*—modak-like sweets made of coconut and jaggery.

In recent years, this chore has been delegated to my wife, and the responsibility of driving her there has shifted from my father to me.

Either her half-century of devotion or her cooking—one of these has definitely pleased the elephant-headed God (I suspect it's the latter). He always ensures low traffic, zero queues, and quick passage for her. Perhaps He has developed a liking for the Kerala delicacy, the *koikattai*, because this year, when the battery in my phone—set with an early morning alarm—died out overnight, He sent a whole platoon of birds of all shapes and sizes to create a din of tweets and twitters right outside my window. Acting as a natural alarm clock, they woke us up exactly on schedule.

While my mother spends a length of time entreating the idol with a year's worth of prayers, my father and I usually wander off and find a spot to sit and wait. This spot is usually beside an ancient well next to the temple. A rusty old board once proudly proclaimed that the tortoise living in that well was over a hundred years old.

That board doesn't exist anymore. Today, the well is covered up like a steel tank. This is the story of how that came to be.

Many years ago, on one such trip, I was standing beside the open well, carrying my tiny son—then barely able to speak. He was thrilled by my description of the great old tortoise and babbled as only babies can: "Tortse, torse, turtise..." giggling away and peering eagerly into the dark water.

At that moment, my kindly, overburdened father appeared—loaded with garlands, coconuts, and plenty of sweet boxes.

Like all married men, he lacked the heart to say anything to his wife directly, and took this moment of isolation to complain to me about the stupidity of rituals.

"God never asked us to offer coconuts," he grumbled. "Even if we have to, one should be enough! Why this garland of twenty coconuts—which He doesn't even eat? And all these flowers and sweet boxes!"

In a moment of frustration, he turned and hurled one coconut into the dark waters of the well. The very well that boasted a century-old tortoise.

That poor tortoise—who had survived two world wars, a country's partitioning, five central governments—was finally felled by the most innocuous of creations: a coconut.

At that exact moment, the tortoise chose to rise to the surface from its secure depths. And that's when it met its nemesis—the meteor-like coconut—head-on.

That split-second remains unforgettable to four souls in the universe: the poor tortoise, myself, my anguished father, and my shocked baby, who till then believed his grandpa to be the kindest man on Earth, incapable of harming a fly.

We saw the coconut hit the tortoise with a loud *thud*. We saw it back-flip and sink like a stone. We stared at each other in stunned silence. Especially my baby, who could not believe that his Gandhian grandpa was, in fact, a revolutionary in disguise.

We slunk away quietly.

But for the entire ride home, my baby—perched on grandpa's lap and facing him—kept repeating in shocked accusation, "Dada, tortise dum," mimicking a punch with his tiny hand. My mother and wife kept asking what the matter was. My father and I maintained a studied silence.

The following year, we found ourselves again beside the well. This time, it was partially covered with metal sheets and bore a stern new board: *DO NOT THROW ANYTHING INTO THE WELL. ESPECIALLY COCONUTS.*

My son, now a year older, wanted to see the tortoise. My father—standing there grumbling about the heavy metal vessels he was now forced to carry—tried to help him by shifting the covers.

In the melee, the vessel in his hand—slick with oil and syrup from the sweetmeats—slipped and crashed straight into the well.

The poor tortoise, probably half-dead from the previous year's encounter, once again timed its end to perfection. He rose to the water's surface, met the falling steel vessel, and continued rising—this time, only in spirit—to his brand-new heavenly abode.

We exited the place quickly. A habit we had, by then, perfected.

This time, my son too stayed quiet on the return journey.

Today, the well is sealed off like a bunker. Nothing can enter—not even air. Not that there's any need for air anymore. Nothing lives in those dark waters now. The board is gone too.

These days, the three of us—grandfather, father, and son—stand quietly beside the well, waiting for the women of the house to finish their prayers.

But we don't complain.
And we don't peer into the well.

CHAPTER NINE

Life Is A Tough Ball Game: A Philosophical Interlude

Life is like the game of squash.

You aren't even as good as the last point you scored — because there's no guarantee the next point will be yours. You might win it. You might lose it. And the one after that. And the one after that. You could end up losing the game altogether.

In this metaphor, life is also your opponent — indefatigable, skilful, strong, and relentless.

Which means: if you slacken even for a moment, you're done for.

To win a single point, you have to be twice as quick, twice as sharp, twice as strong.

Most importantly, you need mental toughness — to recover from the loss of a point, a game, or even a match.

There will be days when you lose continually.
Your opponent will seem stronger than ever — physically and mentally.
You may be unwell, exhausted, down with fever or pain.
These are the days that test your spirit.
On such days, don't be hard on yourself.
Don't tell yourself you must win everything, every day.

These moments exist for a reason:
To remind you there is no such thing as permanent failure or final defeat.
There are only setbacks. And every setback is a test of your will to survive.

Keep ticking.
Reset your goals.
Don't aim impossibly high — that's a recipe for burnout and despair.
Instead, go after the small wins.
One point.
A long, hard rally.
Win one game in a set of five. Push for two. Narrow the margin of defeat.

You may lose the match. But if your mind is unbroken, you're still a winner.
Look at your opponent — and you'll see. Even in victory, they're not smiling.
Because they know they couldn't break you.

And that's your next lesson: **never lose your cool.**
Don't smash your racket — it's just a tool.
Just like how in life, no one else — not your boss, not your family, not your luck — is responsible for your loss.
Only you are.

Smile at your defeat.
It'll help you see the gaps in your game.

It'll infuriate your opponent — because now they know: you're not done. You've got something special coming.

And you will bounce back.

Slowly, or swiftly.

Because the human mind and body are designed to survive — and to win.

Let that instinct take over.

Trust it.

You'll rebound. And you'll win.

But here's a word of caution.

When things begin going your way, don't get cocky.

One point isn't the match.

Don't let confidence turn into carelessness.

Stay calm.

Keep collecting points.

Games.

Sets.

Matches.

Then do it all again.

Because every point must be played like it's both the first and the last.

You aren't destined to win — or to lose.

Destiny has no part to play.

If you think it does, you've already given up.

The outcome of life — whether a day, a year, or a lifetime — depends entirely on how you play **each point.**

No — **each shot.**

Win that shot.

Win that moment.

Keep your focus tight and unwavering.

That's how you win.

Keep working at it.

Because life, like squash, is an open court — and inside it, a

formidable opponent is always waiting.
And you...
you are only as good as the shot you are about to play.

CHAPTER TEN

LOOK BEFORE YOU REACH

I thought it a good idea to carry along a shower gel to the swimming pool—especially since our club had recently renovated the changing rooms and installed a shiny new jacuzzi and swanky cubicles equipped with hot water for swimmers to shower off.

Feeling heroic after 25 laps (in my own signature style, thank you very much), I strode into an inviting cubicle, towel and shower gel in hand. As I reached for the gel, I realized I'd picked the one my sister had gifted my wife on her trip abroad.

"Soft Japanese floral essence," the label read.

I shrugged. I knew the Japanese well, having conducted many workshops for them over the years. This would be minimalist and mild, I reasoned.

I poured out a generous amount of the gel—(*free hai, aur do bottle hai ghar pe*)—and began vigorously lathering myself, in true Indian style. The Japanese are perfectionists, people after my own heart. I thought generously of them as I felt the special ingredients working wonders on me, along with the *fukat ka* hot water provided by the club.

Indeed, the Japanese are perfectionists. When they create a unique fragrance—soft and mild, made for delicate ladies—they expect it to do its job well. The scent of "soft Japanese floral essence" soon began spreading far and wide. Farther and wider, perhaps, than even the Sony Walkman did.

Its fragrance promised visions of doll-like Japanese beauty to every straight male, two-legged or four, who had ever walked the earth.

I suppose all of them thought the pretty mermaids who usually inhabited the pool had mistakenly wandered into the men's changing room for their shower.

Because when I exited the shower cubicle, standing outside with silly romantic smiles on their faces—and God-alone-knows what images in their minds—was the entire male population of our local club, clearly expecting a half-dressed Japanese beauty to emerge.

Well, they got me.

CHAPTER ELEVEN

MY MOTHER, MY MUMBAI

Strangely, to me, my city—Mumbai, where I've lived most of my life—is personified by my mother. Perhaps it's because she too has spent her entire life here. Or maybe it's because she gave birth to me in a place called Bombay Hospital, forever fusing the two in my mind and memory. But I think there's more to it than just that.

My mother moved to the city of Bombay from Kerala when she was about five years old. That was in 1949. She lived in the heart of the city then—Dadar. Those early years left their mark on her, and in a way, on me too. She was beautiful, and there's proof of that still—fading black-and-white photographs in crumbling albums, clippings from forgotten magazines, and sometimes, in fleeting glimpses from vintage films of the 1950s. Wide boulevards, clean roads, swaying palms, and well-dressed people with gentle manners—those frames remind me of her early days in the spotlight.

Back then, her streets were washed every morning. Her trains and trams were punctual. Her skin was translucent. Her hair, magnificent. My mother's family were once wealthy landlords. Her father—a graduate in the frugal 1920s—held a senior position in a respected multinational company. It shows in her bearing. Regal cheekbones, doe eyes, sharp features, and a quiet poise that refused to fade. Just like Mumbai then—golden beaches, quaint suburbs, and indulgent, easy weather. That goodness rubbed off on the people too. Law-abiding. Community-minded. Inclusive. Crime was rare, and the police were efficient, incorruptible, and respected.

Her cross-cultural background showed in her speech. She spoke what we now call 'Bambaiyya'—a mash-up of Hindi wrapped in Marathi grammar, laced with Gujarati, seasoned with Arabic, and touched with Tamil and Malayalam. It didn't sound elegant, but it was oddly democratic. A Nepali watchman, a Parsi industrialist, his Bihari driver, and a Goan secretary could live out lifetimes talking to each other in it.

Her life revolved around two temples—Siddhivinayak and Mahalakshmi. She tells me stories of visiting the former when He was just a statue under a tree. Her devotion was not just a ritual, it was a schedule. Her calendar, filled with pujas, fasts, and festivals—some even I hadn't heard of—marked her faith. But she remained undaunted, accommodating celebrations from every forgotten state of this country. "These festivals," she tells me, "connect me to the people who make me who I am."

My mother's marriage was cemented in 1964. That year, the city was formally handed over to Maharashtra and anointed its capital. A year later, my sister was born. The family spent a few years in Delhi, before returning in 1970. That's when I was born.

Those early years are my favorite. I'd wager there wasn't a more beautiful place on Earth than Mumbai in the '70s.

She had the glow of a young mother, still in her prime, and I was completely smitten. I remember her fragrance, the feel of her soft, welcoming soil, her damp sari that was so comforting when I lay on her lap. Her flushed laughter when she told me stories. These are my sweetest memories.

But time has a way of catching up—with mothers and with cities.

The decades that followed saw her struggling to keep pace with change. She drew inward, surrounded herself with family, retreating from a world whose values had shifted. The unholy nexus between politics and crime tore into the city. Her children—married, educated—began drifting away.

Age takes a toll on mothers. Especially on those who've given everything away. And mine gave it all. Maybe she should have taken more care of herself. But when floods, riots, terrorism, and grief come wave after wave, even the strongest begin to break. My sister passed away after a long, hard battle. And that kind of loss is never easy on any mother.

She's still beautiful. But now, it's a quiet, subdued kind of beauty—peaceful, detached. She does her best for us. We do what we can for her. She doesn't complain. She still has her little joys. Like the Mumbai Metro—what a lovely thing that is. She loves it. More of it may make a difference. Maybe.

But deep inside, I know the clock cannot be turned back. Her lines are beautiful, but they are lines on her face. The rain may wash away the grime for a while, but the potholes remain. The doctors are there, but so are the diseases.

Still, I stay. I walk her streets, hold her hand. Sometimes we sit together and talk about all the wonderful times we had. And in the quietest hours, under a pink and crimson sky, when the sun's rays are gentle and forgiving, some of the pain eases. Time stands still for my mother. And for her son, who loves her so much.

Part 3

CHAPTER TWELVE

THE BULLFIGHT

How poetic is this bullfight,
    In the middle he stands in might,
    Handsome, chivalrous, dressed in black,
    Great in heart, grace in fight,
    Our hero! This champion built like granite!
    But how strange is this, lonely is he,
    The crowd roots for his enemy!
    That frail-looking man dressed in tights,
    With cloaks and daggers and razzmatazz.
    He steps about on ginger toes,
    Makes mockery of our great hero,
    With horses, spears, and sharpened sticks,
    He attacks and tears our hero bit by bit.
    The crowd, intent, cheers his blows—
    This unfair fight of man versus hero.
    They clap to see our hero bleed,
    His step is slow, his senses reel.
    But heroes are not one and all—
    Our hearty champ soon wins his crown.
    In a breath, he brings him to a crawl,
    Quivering in fear, white overall.
    Those great muscles hide a generous heart,

He snorts contempt, lets his foe depart.
The crowd aghast, the matador silent,
Our hero departs, once for all.
Dark is the night, the ring pin-drop quiet,
The hero is stretched, at peace, at rest.
The God of War alights from the sky:
"He's earned his right to the pantheon.
For in the day, he was the better man—
The only human in the bullfight."

CHAPTER THIRTEEN

Escape from Makhbarabad

My bus screeched to a dramatic halt at the town square of Makhbarabad—a move seemingly designed to jolt awake all its half-asleep, uncomfortable passengers. I shivered in the early morning cold as I stepped off with my small overnight bag, heading towards the cluster of hotels on the fringes of the bus stand. They all looked the same—worn, uninspired, and indistinguishable.

For 200 bucks, I secured a smelly, bug-infested room. One look at the stained bed and pillow was enough to kill any desire to lie down. Whatever traces of sleep remained were soon blasted away by an icy shower—a few reluctant trickles of freezing water from a crooked, leaky tap, into a moss-coated iron bucket.

I felt trapped.

Just two days ago, I was a carefree youth fresh out of college, living the dream—waking up at noon, watching MTV, playing cricket, zooming around on bikes till midnight, and topping it off with jam sessions alongside my equally aimless friends.

To pacify my parents, I'd pretend to scan the jobs section of the newspaper and dutifully apply to a dozen roles. I didn't care if those resumes vanished into a void. I had zero desire to work—truthfully, I had no idea what I wanted to do with my life and preferred not to think about it. Thankfully, my friends felt the same way. My parents, though bewildered by their grown-up son, were too polite to ask questions—perhaps comforted by my seemingly diligent, albeit futile, application process.

I only applied to big-name companies—perfect props for my soliloquies on why I "deserved the best." In reality, I counted on being rejected so I could keep skating through life without any pesky responsibilities.

But one company didn't play by the script.

This one was a rising star in consumer electronics, creating ripples in the market, building international alliances, and earning headlines. The kind of place every middle-class father would beam about. And now, this corporate prodigy had thrown a spanner in my freewheeling world by inviting me for a written test and interview.

Makhbarabad? What the hell kind of place was that?

My mother cheerily pointed out that it was just 6–8 hours from Bombay by road or rail. Perfect, she beamed—I could work there weekdays and still come home for long weekends. Somehow, her optimism about my future didn't fill me with the same enthusiasm. I mumbled something about hurdles still remaining, but before I could explain, she had already skipped off to the temple with coconuts for the deity who had dared to answer her prayers.

So here I was—in India's shining beacon of progress: Makhbarabad. Where emperors had begun their careers and industrialists had forged their empires. I had no desire to be either. A rockstar or even a VJ sounded infinitely more appealing.

It wasn't even 7 a.m. I flicked on the TV in search of Classic Rock. No MTV. No Star TV. Just one dismal cable channel belting out *bhakti sangeet*—devotional songs for the spiritually devoted at sunrise. Saffron-clad men beat drums tunelessly while trudging up a mountain. The video cut to a bearded singer with bulging, frog-like eyes screaming accusations at sinners. Scorched by his gaze, I promptly switched it off.

Fed up with the idiot box, I tiptoed down the rancid-smelling staircase to the reception and roused the sleeping clerk sprawled across the lobby's sole sofa. After much coaxing and some well-placed prodding, he finally got up and grudgingly served me a bitter cup of tea.

Lingering at the hotel was pointless, so I caught a rickshaw to the factory where the interviews were scheduled. I had no idea where it was, but since Makhbarabad consisted of roughly five streets, I assumed I'd be there in 20 minutes.

The auto driver, clearly familiar with the place, spat out a mouthful of tobacco and zoomed off at a pace that made my teeth rattle. I looked out uneasily as Makhbarabad's cramped chaos gave way to the desolate sprawl of rural India. The road deteriorated into what looked like a tractor path, loosely held together by bits of tar.

Cotton farms gave way to sugarcane fields, then to paddy. Dread swelled inside me—what I had imagined to be a quick jaunt was turning into a full-blown expedition. After nearly two hours, the factory finally loomed ahead. My heart sank when I saw the cluster of staff quarters around it. A quick word with the watchman confirmed my fears—this was indeed where employees lived.

A perfect study in isolation—miles from even Makhbarabad.

With half an hour to go before the test, I decided to explore. Several employees were already heading into the canteen, so I tagged along. The canteen resembled an assembly line, which probably comforted the factory workers but felt cold and impersonal to me. Metal tables stretched in rows. People sat silently, eating whatever was doled out, without a word.

No one paid me the slightest attention. Any attempts at small talk were met with blank stares. Two Japanese (or Korean?) men sat across from me, surrounded by senior officials acting like a buffer. The visitors seemed uninterested in the company. I offered a hopeful smile, but the inscrutable duo looked right through me.

Maybe the place had gotten to them too.

I trudged silently to the examination hall, which was packed with candidates—unlike me, they seemed genuinely thrilled to be here. To them, this job was as thrilling as space travel. They nervously eyed one another. Nerd central. Heavy glasses, heavier books, clothes that seemed a decade out of fashion—they were battling it out for King of the Nerds.

They stared when they saw me. I was an octopus in a turtle tank. From whispered conversations, I gathered they idolized someone called Mr. Goregaonkar—their rockstar. He was head of R&D, had studied abroad, collected multiple PhDs, and been featured in local newspapers. Apparently, that was enough to earn their Grammy.

I twiddled my thumbs in boredom. I must have nodded off because the guy next to me nudged me awake. "Look! Goregaonkar is here!"

I expected a sharp, suited, foreign-returned professional. Instead, a portly man with oily hair, bell-bottoms, and rubber chappals waddled in. This was the hero. In a booming voice, he declared how fortunate we were to be shortlisted. He detailed the rigor of the upcoming tests and interviews—which he himself would personally conduct!

Then came the perks: accommodation at the staff quarters, free meals in the canteen, daily evening prayers at the on-site temple, and weekend escapades to Makhbarabad for "entertainment." The nerds reacted like he was offering them a lifetime in Vegas.

I felt dizzy. Axl Rose was being elbowed out by Goregaonkar. Cricket replaced by evening prayers. Rock concerts traded for rickety auto rides. Jam sessions swapped for staring at stars and listening to village dogs argue. The test began, but my mind was spinning.

Interviews were scheduled for the next day. I exited slowly. The others vanished—probably off to cram some more. I admired their focus but couldn't see myself saying a single meaningful word to any of them, ever. A lifetime of conversation with this bunch could be written on the back of a bus ticket.

Back in Makhbarabad, I couldn't face my grimy hotel room again. The thought of a Bollywood movie cheered me up slightly. The local theatre was screening a flop starring Aditya Pancholi and a forgettable starlet. The theatre reeked of stale sweat, the seats were broken, and mine was half-hinged, rocking me sideways and forward unpredictably.

"I can't say I'm not having a rocking time in Makhbarabad," I thought bitterly.

The film began—and then the lights went out. Power cut. No one seemed to care. The crowd was completely disinterested. Maybe that explained the lack of decent films. This one didn't deserve attention anyway. It was bad enough to make the hotel bedbugs seem welcoming.

Suddenly, something warm brushed against my feet. I jumped—rat?! But no, it was a scrawny dog, munching boldly on the samosa in my hand. He wagged his tail and looked at me with mournful eyes. The first friendly face I'd met in Makhbarabad. I handed him the rest of my samosa and stepped out.

It was already dark. The shops were shut, lights off, streets deserted. Just 8 p.m., and the town was in a coma. I thought of my friends in Bombay. Div, Sarosh, Bosco—by now they'd be on their third pitcher at Café New York. The jukebox would be playing *Hotel California*. Later, they'd head to Sarosh's place and belt out *Wish You Were Here* in my memory.

I wandered the streets, picturing the life that lay ahead if I stayed. Bhajans replacing rock, Aditya Pancholi subbing for Arnold, missal pav instead of kebabs. A life behind bars before the crime had even begun.

I reached the town square, lost in thought. And there it was—a single bus belching black fumes. A lifeline. A miracle. A greasy, coughing savior.

The conductor leaned outside, scanning for last-minute stragglers. Something inside me snapped. I ran to him. "Where does this go?"

"Bombay."

"Seat?"

"Middle seat. Last row."

"I'll take it! Just give me one minute—I'll grab my bag!"

I tore back to the hotel, faster than I've ever run. I even tipped the receptionist. I must've been the happiest person ever to ride that bumpy middle seat in the last row of a bus.

When I climbed up the stairs to our apartment, dawn hadn't yet broken. My poor mom was outside, diligently drawing the *kollam* like she did every morning. She looked up, startled. Before she could say a word, I dropped down and stretched myself full-length at her feet. She was too stunned to speak.

I pleaded with her—promising that if she didn't scold me or send me away, I'd change my life. I'd find a job, take care of her, and never leave her side again. She just stared at me in disbelief, not saying a word.

As for me, I slipped back into my life. But every time I got really high, my mind would wander back to Makhbarabad... and that one memory never failed to bring me crashing back to earth. Real fast.

CHAPTER FOURTEEN

BREAKUP NOTE

Goodbye. Walking away from a relationship of two decades is never easy. Especially one in which we were so completely into each other.

Although you came into my life gradually, you'd admit I left no stone unturned in wooing you. Chocolates, sweets, beer, the best grub my thin wallet could afford—you got it all. Maybe that's how you got spoilt.

At first, you dulled. Then your beauty began to fall apart. No cosmetic could hide the sallow color or the deep ridges and cracks spreading across you.

The last five years were a drag. Neither of us cared anymore, but we felt each other's presence—miserably, irritably. We couldn't stand each other, could we?

Things got very painful. Long stretches of nothing between us. You were hurting, and all you did was hurt me. From morning to night, you dished out misery. I doubt that gave you much joy. You wouldn't even let me sleep, poking me constantly with your little digs.

I tried. Tried to fix things, to drain the venom that had taken over. But there wasn't much left to salvage. Finally, we were advised to part ways. I gave it six more months. But the canker was too deep.

I always knew it would be painful. I knew you'd lash out, and there'd be blood. You tore into me. I said nothing. It took all I had not to scream. The pain was terrible—I saw stars. Not figuratively. I saw their contours. I saw every explosion on their surface.

Just when I thought I'd pass out, the dentist held up your broken half and said,

"The bitch just refused to come out. One stubborn helluva wisdom tooth, she is. She's broken off at the root and will now be stuck to you forever—unless you want an operation to cut her out."

I staggered away, clutching my jaw.

A chip off the old block?

Or is it the other way around?

CHAPTER FIFTEEN

Justice Of The Highest Order

'*Perutashi Sanikaramai*'—the Saturdays in the Tamil month of *Perutashi*—are considered especially auspicious for devotees of Lord Balaji. So, the Balaji temple at Fanaswadi was packed with fellow Tamilians of every kind, eager to solicit favors from the all-powerful protector. I was there too—as escort cum driver for my dear mother.

The temple sanctum was divided equally into two halves: one for males and the other for ladies. One inhabitant among the packed ladies' side drew everyone's attention. Standing almost a head taller than the rest was a eunuch. Draped in a saree, with devotion etched into her face, she stood leaning on a tripod walking-stick, her eyes fixed in steadfast concentration on the idol—whose black stone complexion appeared no different from that of this ardent devotee.

She seemed to be a regular at the temple, chatting freely in Tamil with the priest, who inquired after her with genuine familiarity.

A hush fell over the crowd as the priest solemnly performed the *aarti*, then took his time circulating it along with the *abhishekam* among the devotees waiting patiently in the sanctum.

Finally, the priest removed the tiny flower garlands that had adorned the Lord—meant to be distributed only among the ladies, as per tradition. Slowly, he moved around, handing out the garlands to eager women, who would quickly pin the divine token to their hair before stepping back into the fast-paced world waiting at the temple gates.

Soon, only two of us were left to receive the last garland.

One was the eunuch, waiting with sublime faith in her eyes.

And then there was me, waiting opportunistically for any extra benefit I could get—*free of cost*.

"Neither of us is a woman," I thought. "So, who would he give it to?"

The priest approached with the final garland in hand. For once, doubt clouded his eyes—he had a difficult choice to make. On one hand stood a well-dressed man, clearly from a respectable family. On the other, a poor eunuch. A pariah. Neither man nor woman. Not considered a member of regular society. Existing in its darkest fringes. Often treated worse than an animal.

Both our hands were stretched out. The priest hesitated; the garland held just inches above ours.

Then—a sudden gust of wind blew through the sanctum. And the tiny garland slipped from his hand.

Into **hers**.

As I watched her hobble away, a huge smile of utter happiness creasing her face, for a moment she looked truly beautiful in the soft light of the temple *diyas*.

It struck me then: while the Supreme Court of this timeless nation may still debate matters of sexual identity and the rights of such individuals, there seemed to be no doubt in the mind of the **Creator** who made us all.

In **His** universe, there's a place for every one of His creatures.

And He ensures they all get their due—and leave His court feeling happy and content.

CHAPTER SIXTEEN

THE CROOKED ROAD TO HEALTH

Run. Don't run. Walk. It's better. Don't walk in the mornings, there's too much smog in the air. Walking in the evenings isn't good for digestion and there must be at least a 3-hour gap between walking and bedtime. Play. But don't play impact sports. Those would cause permanent damage to your knees and joints. Swim. But remember the water in most pools are not clean and will lead to skin damage.

In any case, exercise does not really matter. Your diet does. Breakfast, like a King, lunch like a prince and dinner like a pauper. That's bullshit. Eat 5 times a day in small equal quantities. No. Focus on proteins. Eat white meat, avoid red meat. Eat only fish. Eat only chicken. Eat only eggs. make that only the egg white. That's a recipe for high cholesterol! Eat only fruits, veggies. Eat only leafy veggies. don't eat leafy veggies because they have worm eggs in them. Avoid other veggies they have high carbs and lead to gas attacks. Eat that ugly looking Brazilian jungle vegetable, it cures cancer. No avoid it! it leads to impotence. Stick to fruits but avoid the skin. No eat only the skin, they're rich in proteins. But don't eat the fruits which have red seeds they are poisonous and green fruits should be avoided if they were purple flowers.

Drink milk. But not buffalo milk, drink cow's milk. But make it skimmed. No skimmed is processed, drink goat milk, no camel milk. Don't drink milk! the body cannot digest milk after the age of three. Drink mother's milk? only till three.

Drink? Water. But not from the tap. Mineral water. Which is tap water only dirtier. No, only water from the Alps. Drinking is good. Small quantity of alcohol helps keep the arteries from clogging. But drink only wine. Red wine. but only with white meat. But now, since no white meat, there can't be no wine. Drink only coffee and tea. No, they cause damage over the long run. Drink green tea. No it causes prostrate problems.

Don't smoke! it causes cancer. Smoke cigars less tar. Beedis are better. But cause ulcer. Smoking up is best. Pot is bad. It is medicine. Yogis smoke up. Yogi's go nowhere. Breathing the air in any city is equivalent to smoking 20 cigarettes.

Welcome to the age of information. You are now better informed about every aspect of your health and can take informed decisions about leading a healthier, happier and emotionally stable life.

(This article I first wrote 12 years ago on June 6, 2013 on my blog, then I shared it as a comment in The Economist, under my pen name http://www.economist.com/comment/ 2395461#comment-2395461 This became very popular and got reproduced in different languages across the world. Must have been something I ate that day.)

CHAPTER SEVENTEEN

THE SYMBOL OF LOVE

"C'mon Zennie wake up! It's time for school!" Yelled mama.

Zennie got up with a start. She was forgetting something. The word, 'school' had suddenly triggered something in her mind that reminded her with a start that she had missed telling her mom or doing an important thing.

Usually, Zennie would skip and hop her way to school. Or at least till the school bus that picked her up from the lane in which her apartment block was located.

But today the dreadful thought that she was forgetting something important, robbed the hop, skip and jump from her step.

"Wassup Zennie, why're you dragging your feet today?" queried her father who usually walked her to the school bus.

"Waaahh!" wailed Zennie suddenly, lifting her arms, indicating to her father that she wanted to be carried.

"Well ok!" said her father in astonishment, "What's gotten into you today? Are you well?"

He quickly touched her forehead.

No sign of fever.

Zennie had meanwhile locked her head on his shoulder and was moodily silent.

"Well, here's your bus, well in time." said her father as he attempted to put her down on the ground.

"Waaah!" Wailed Zennie suddenly, "I don't want to go to school!"

"That's not happening." Said her father firmly as he handed her over to the female attendant in the bus.

Zennie retreated to a corner of the bus and sat quietly throughout the ride, the tear drops on her cheeks, glinted in the light of the morning sun.

Slowly she followed the other children as they made their way into school and trudged on her tiny legs to her classroom, where 25 other children sat in what was the first step of their long journey in education.

She approached her desk and sat down petulantly. Her palms cupping her little face as she tried to figure out, the mixture of emotions, feelings and thoughts that coursed through her mind.

She hated everything!

She hated school. She hated her classroom. She hated drawing.

And most of all she hated Riya Multani.

In one instant her happy world had been shattered by Riya Multani.

Riya Multani. The smiling, pretty little girl who got delicious pastries in her dabba.

Riya Multani, with her long, silken brown hair that bounced like daisies every time she shook her head.

Riya Multani. The teacher's favourite.

Riya Multani. The girl who...

The thought of it pained her.

Too young to understand what she was feeling, Zennie began wailing loudly.

"Mama chahiye!"

"Kya hua Zennie, why are you crying?"

It was Asher.

There was a concerned look on his angelic face, crowned by light brown curling hair, which made her heart lurch.

Usually, the sight of him, would make her utterly happy and she would start giggling and talking at the same time.

They'd begin talking almost immediately as he took his place next to her. The day would be forgotten, the teacher would be forgotten, the sun, rain, mom, dad and everything else would be forgotten. They had so much to talk about and do together.

Every morning, they would greet each other, in the simple endearing ways that only children can. They would exchange tales, tall and short, impressing each other with stories that their young minds had only partly understood.

"Patah hai, when I grow up, I'm going to be a pistol shooter and win a bronze medal!"

"I like only bronze medal. Which medal do you want?"

"Bronze for me too. I don't want gold."

"You know yesterday, Liu doggie played catch-catch with my ball. She liked my ball so much, she wanted to take it home."

Life was so good back then. Life was so much fun.

She, Asher and their little world.

But today, everything had changed.

A shadow loomed over her happiness.

A shadow called Riya Multani.

Pretty, plump, fair, brown & bouncy-haired Riya Multani with the wonder water-bottle from USA.

Zennie suddenly found herself disliking everything about Riya Multani.

From her pink, plump cheeks. To her water bottle, to her tinny laugh.

Oh, why had that Riya Multani come into her life, into her class, into her school?

And stolen from her, her happy little world.

Taken away from her, the things meant for her.

Snatched from her, his heart.

Asher's heart.

The heart that he had so caringly drawn (with Zennie's help!)

Red and beautiful.

The teacher had told them to draw anything they wanted and gift it to someone in their class.

Zennie had drawn a ball for Asher, because she knew he loved football.

Then quietly she had peeked over his hand to see what he was drawing.

It was a heart!

Somehow Asher had got the shape right, but was struggling with the colours.

Zennie looked at her crayons and picked out the perfect red (the one she loved) and gave it to Asher for colouring.

For the next half an hour or so, he coloured in rapt attention, pink tongue jutting out from between his teeth.

Zennie kept her one eye on him. Making sure to hand him his water bottle. Giving him a few bits of chips from her dabba.

All of this he drank and ate without once wandering from his task.

Zennie felt a warm glow spreading over her tiny chest. She leaned over and whispered, "It's beautiful!"

He looked up distracted, and smiled, "I hope she likes it!"

Zennie felt her heart sing. It was as though a whole romantic musical was playing out in front of her.

And when the teacher asked them to hand over their work to the person, they'd made it for in the class, Zennie quickly handed the ball to Asher waiting for him to hand over his heart.

But there was an anti-climax awaiting little Zennie!

He got up and ran to Riya Multani's desk and handed it over to her.

Riya Multani blushed.

Zennie burst out crying.

Asher looked confused.

That was yesterday.

But now he had a concerned look on his little face.

"Baaah!" wailed Zennie even louder, catching the attention of her teacher.

"Oh Zennie! Come here...What happened, why are you crying dear? Someone said something to you?"

Zennie trudged up to her and tried to explain the confused state of her mind through her tears.

"Miss, miss, Asher drew the heart..."

"Yes dear, Asher drew the heart."

"Waah! HeartHegaveRiyaMultani...waaah!"

"What? What? Speak slowly dear!"

"Waah! HeartHegaveRiyaMultani...waaah!"

"Heart? who gave heart? Your heart? What?"

"Waaah!"

"Stop it! Stop it. Say slowly."

"Miss, Asher made heart..."

"Yes, yes"

"My colour red..."

"You gave your crayon…"

"Waah! HegaveRiyaMultani! Waaah!"

"Stop it! Asher gave your crayon to Riya Multani?"

"No waah! Heart!"

"Stop stop, Asher gave your heart? No, it was his heart dear. I saw him draw it!"

"Wah!"

"Zennie dear, why are *you* crying, if Asher gave *his* heart to *Riya*?"

The nickel dropped in the teacher's head.

"How cute is this!" she thought to herself. She'd noticed Zennie and Asher were mostly together. Now it all made sense.

"Asher come here please. Why did you give your heart to Riya Multani? Why didn't you give it to your best friend, Zennie?"

Zennie too had stopped sobbing and was looking up at Asher with wide teary eyes.

Not knowing what to say, Asher rolled his eyes and lifted his hand.

On his wrist was the single gold thread that Zennie had innocently tied, a few days earlier, when the class was celebrating the festival of Raksha Bandhan.

Part 4

CHAPTER EIGHTEEN

WITH FRIENDS LIKE THESE

Sometimes, silence is indeed golden. Especially if one is celebrating a *golden anniversary*—fifty years of togetherness. What an occasion!

Recently, I was part of the audience at one such event. All of us gazed in quiet awe at the shy, wrinkled couple on stage, squinting into the lights and blinking slowly, their eyes ringed with cataract. Our collective imagination went into overdrive.

We thought of the years of struggle. Of the husband toiling endlessly to build a secure life. Of the wife, waiting up every night, then waking early to care for her in-laws, her siblings, the household. We imagined the stress she bore so her husband wouldn't have to. The sacrifices. The love. The shared pain. Fifty years of it.

It was a beautiful moment—until their well-meaning friends and relatives got the mic.

The compère invited people on stage to share stories about the couple. And that's when things took a *turn*.

The Destruction Begins

First up: the bride's younger sister. A recently retired school principal. No stranger to the mic—and clearly no fan of brevity. She launched into a long monologue about her 35-year career before finally arriving at the couple. The audience had already begun nodding off by then—except for the couple on stage, who were probably fast asleep.

Then came the real bombs.

She described how, fifty years ago, the groom came to their house to see her sister. The bride, she noted helpfully, was "very fat." The groom's mother apparently muttered this observation aloud, to which the father responded, "Well, our son is as black as a stormy night." That's how the union began: with a loud compromise.

She then mentioned how lucky her sister was in marriage—because she "never had to do any work." The poor mother-in-law cooked every day, even dipped her finger in the coffee to check the temperature (she was "very hygienic," the speaker assured us). The audience flinched. And then came the kicker: the groom too never worked much, having been the pampered only child of wealthy parents.

You could feel the collective reimagining in the audience. The couple who once seemed heroic now appeared... well, *coddled*.

More Revelations

Enter sister number two. She proudly shared how her sister never stepped out of the house—except to the temple next door. After their in-laws passed away, the husband did all the grocery shopping. She fondly recalled running into him at the market, gossiping away as he picked vegetables.

She mentioned how her elder sister would summon them over during festivals—not for company, but to help with chores. The principal and she would slog, while their elder sister relaxed, her talent for delegation fully intact.

And then, almost gleefully, she spoke of how the brother-in-law loved taking his "pretty, slim" sisters-in-law on weekend picnics. "Come, my dears, let's enjoy the weekend," he'd say.

The old man on stage shrank into his chair. The wife looked around, possibly scanning for the nearest table to crawl under.

Friends Who Meant Well

The groom, desperate to restore some dignity, asked his friends to share a few words. Big mistake.

One friend—also a neighbour—thanked him on behalf of their society. Why? Because the old man had ensured smooth water supply by managing the pump room. A *model pump man*, he declared. He even worked "day and night," never took money.

Mumbaikars in the audience frowned. *Which society in Mumbai ever had water 24/7?* This wasn't praise. It was a demotion.

Then came the final blow: their oldest friend. He spoke of a movie where an elderly couple is gifted a honeymoon suite by their kids. "When we had the youth, we lacked the facilities," they say. "Now we have the facilities but not the vigour." Turning to the couple, he chuckled, "Hope your kids haven't booked you a suite. Clearly, *vigour* is in short supply."

The Aftermath

By now, the couple was visibly shattered. They barely looked at each other. If they were regretting anything, it wasn't the marriage—it was this celebration, and their decision to *hand over the mic.*

They got up abruptly, announced lunch early, and tried to disappear into the crowd. The audience, of course, forgot everything once the biryani arrived.

The golden glow of the moment had been replaced by a rather *dull copperish* one. But hey, at least the lunch was good.

CHAPTER NINETEEN

A FATHER'S GIFT

A few days ago, my parents dropped by to celebrate Holi with us. My father quietly took me aside and handed me a new shirt.

"This is for you, from me," he said.

It's a white shirt with tiny blue checks. A very pretty shirt, from a renowned international designer.

It's been a long time since my father bought me a shirt.

There was a time when he used to get me shirts regularly. I must have been about sixteen then, in junior college. Branded shirts weren't available in India back in those days, and if you didn't have a good tailor (I didn't), your shirt would usually turn out boxy, with stiff collars and awkward shoulders. T-shirts were a luxury that middle-class boys like me couldn't really afford.

Perhaps my father understood the silent turmoil of his teenage son. Or maybe he simply wanted to give me the best he could. Whatever his reason, he began to scour the Fort area of Bombay (as it was known then), where he worked. He discovered that street hawkers there sold imported, factory-reject shirts—mostly from Hong Kong and Taiwan—at affordable prices.

These shirts were superbly stitched and well-made. If you had the patience to sift through the mountains of options, you could find a gem or two. My father had that patience. More importantly, he had an immense love for his son. Soon, he began bringing home some truly wonderful shirts, and I remained in smart company right through college.

I remember all of them, vividly.

The first was a full-sleeve shirt with minuscule grey checks. That remains my favorite shirt to this day. I don't think I've ever felt better—or looked better—in anything else.

The only issue? The sleeves were too short. They ended about three inches above my wrist.

My father and I would joke that perhaps the Chinese had shorter arms, which is why their sleeves were like that. But I didn't mind. I'd roll them up and wear the shirt almost twice a week.

Then there were the others:

A white one with blue lines.

A thick green-striped slim-fit.

A baggy shirt with thin green-black stripes.

And a shiny white one with almost-full sleeves.

Of course, a shirt can only do so much. My father knew that looking good also meant taking care of the body inside the shirt.

He had a bull-bar installed at home and pushed me to go running every morning. Since my college started early, he would wake me up at the crack of dawn, ready with a glass of milk—into which he would break two raw eggs, sweetened with a spoonful of honey—and gently coax me into gulping it down.

He even visited me at my hostel during my first year. I still remember the disappointment on his face as he took in my shabby clothes and disheveled look—products of hostel life and careless grooming. Stung by that expression, I made it a point to stay well turned-out for the rest of my time there.

Years later, when I started working, he insisted on buying me my first set of work clothes. I tried to protest—telling him mine was a sales job and good clothes wouldn't last in Bombay's humid weather. But he wouldn't hear of it.

So off we went to Charag Din, one of the few premium men's stores in Bombay at the time. There, he bought me a fine pair of trousers and four beautifully tailored shirts.

Then, as if to mark a milestone, he took me to Kemps Corner. A premium brand called Louis Philippe had just entered India and opened a showroom there.
That's where he bought me my first shirt costing over Rs. 1,000.

It was a stunner—virgin white with thin red lines. That shirt never failed me. It helped me crack every sales pitch, every interview, every management school presentation. It put me in the good books of clients and bosses alike.

Wearing my father's shirts throughout my life has felt like being cloaked in his blessings. Much like Karna in the Mahabharata, who wore the divine armor gifted by his father, Surya—the Sun God—and was made invincible.

Today, I'm trying on this new shirt my father has just given me. It fits perfectly, except for the sleeve, which is short by about an inch.

But that doesn't bother me.
I'll roll up the sleeves.
And I can't wait to go out into the world wearing it.

Rose By Another Name

Prakash squeezed himself between the window and the sleeping man, settling down on the hard wooden plank that doubled as the seat, bed, and table — the all-purpose furniture of every second-class compartment on passenger trains that crisscrossed the country.

It was unbearably hot and stuffy. Worse, the compartment was overcrowded.

So focused was he on grabbing his seat and wedging in his luggage, that he hadn't spared a thought for his family as they fought their way through the jostling crowd. It was only after sinking into the narrow recess between his lolling neighbor and the sun-baked wooden interior of the train that his mind finally began to disengage.

And remember them.

His overweight wife had somehow forced her way into the same compartment. After much wailing and elbowing with other contenders, she'd managed to plant herself and their two children in the seat facing his.

The children — both under five — wore that familiar dull, emancipated look that far too many Indian children do. The kind that comes from being underfed and underloved.

Prakash's eyes drifted to his wife — and he barely managed to hide his disgust.

God! How she'd let herself go.

He remembered her as pretty — downright beautiful, in fact — when they got married. Slim, glowing. He'd even proudly changed her maiden name, as was the custom, to match that of the reigning Bollywood queen of the time.

But fifteen years, two late children, and a lifetime of dashed fortunes had smudged all that beauty into something shapeless. Her sari was shabby and poorly draped. Her hair, limp and greasy. The flesh sagged from her cheeks, her face was ringed with dark circles, and her dull skin gave her a permanently exhausted look.

If only I'd known she'd turn into this, he thought bitterly. Worse — bring along the curse she was born with. He was certain: every misfortune in his life could be traced back to her. His inability to hold a job. His failed business ventures. Even the years they'd spent trying to conceive.

This woman is a burden I've been saddled with. And today, she might very well be the reason I get thrown in jail.

A chill ran up his spine.

He had managed to secure tickets for himself and the kids. But hers — that was another matter. It was a borrowed ticket, arranged at the last minute by a shady agent. A real gamble.

Either be caught ticketless, or use someone else's valid ticket.

He had chosen the latter. Not that it was much of a choice.

The problem? The ticket belonged to a 25-year-old woman of another religion. And his wife — well, she was fifteen years older and looked older still. No Ticket Collector (TC) worth his salt would miss it, especially not in this parochial stretch of the country.

25! Who was he kidding? There was no way they'd get away with this. He could already see himself spending the night behind bars.

The train had left the station a while ago, and as if on cue, he caught sight of the TC in the next compartment.

Middle-aged, scraggly-bearded, and gruff — the man looked like someone who'd skipped a shave and a smile for years. He barked orders, coughed with deep tobacco-ravaged lungs, and with a sinewy arm, pulled two ticketless travelers out by the scruff of their necks.

This man meant business.

"This fat sow will be the end of me," Prakash muttered, casting a look at his trembling wife, who now seemed to grasp the gravity of their situation. Her eyes were wide with panic.

Suddenly, an idea struck him.

He pressed the fake ticket into her hand and quickly yanked the children over to his side.

It took only a moment for her to understand. He was disowning her.

He had the real tickets for himself and the kids. All legal. And that meant she would be left alone, holding a ticket that didn't belong to her — a ticket that could land her in jail for impersonation.

Her eyes filled with horror as the realization hit.

She began pleading, her voice breaking, begging him to save her. She clutched at his arm, desperate and sobbing.

But he turned away, hard-faced. He snarled at their stunned children to look away too.

Before the other passengers could fully grasp the wickedness unfolding, the TC had arrived.

His sharp, fiery eyes scanned the compartment like searchlights.

Beneath the brim of his peaked cap, his red, dry eyes blazed. A great beak of a nose tore out from his unkempt beard, and between yellowing tobacco-stained teeth, thin cruel lips curled with contempt.

The other passengers, mostly simple folk, shrank under his gaze. No one moved. No one spoke.

Prakash handed over his and the children's tickets, ignoring his wife's choked sobs.

She looked up at the TC, hands trembling, and passed him the fake ticket.

A heavy sob escaped her as her sari slipped from her face.

Their eyes met. And she shrank involuntarily, in shame and fear.

The TC barely glanced at the ticket before another ticketless traveler tried sneaking past.

With a snarl, the TC sprang into action — leaping over benches, grabbing the man by the collar just as he lunged for the door.

Pandemonium broke loose.

The man's companions tried to flee, along with other ticketless passengers, but the TC was everywhere — barking, shoving, dragging people back.

It took him some time, but he eventually brought order to the chaos.

When the train pulled into the next station, he jumped off with the errant passengers in tow and a smug look on his face.

Prakash sat frozen, pale with dread.

His wife sobbed quietly. Some of the other women tried to comfort her. But none could hide the contempt they felt for Prakash.

His wife had quietened now. Resigned, it seemed. The train jerked back to life and began rolling forward like a tired elephant.

Then, just as it began gathering speed, a sudden shout startled her.

She turned to the window. It was the TC.

Seeing him appear again hit Prakash like a punch to the gut.

The TC was holding something.

It was the ticket.

The very ticket he'd taken from Prakash's wife.

Prakash winced, expecting damnation.

But instead, the TC ran alongside the moving train, reached in through the window, and handed the ticket to her.

"You'll need to show this to the other TCs," he managed to rasp before letting go and collapsing onto the platform.

She stared at the ticket, her hands tightening around it.

And just like that, a quiet calm washed over her — a strange new dignity.

She held on to it, this time not out of fear, but with purpose.

And as each new TC came by, none of them raised an eyebrow. The ticket was valid.

By the time they reached their destination the next morning, Prakash's fear had given way to something else — curiosity.

As they made their slow way out of the station, he snatched the ticket from her hand.

"Give me that," he barked.

He looked down — and froze.

This wasn't the same ticket.

Somewhere in the chaos, the ticket must've gotten swapped.

This one belonged to a woman named "Ritu Prasad."

A woman of the same age as his wife. No wonder no one had questioned it.

The name tugged at something in the back of his mind.

But then he saw an empty autorickshaw and charged toward it, his thoughts of "Ritu Prasad" lost in the urgency of grabbing a ride.

The woman who was once *Ritu Prasad* paused for a moment to look back at the departing train.

At its very end, in the tiny window of the guard's compartment, stood the TC.

Cap in hand.

He watched her.

Just as he had twenty years ago, when he'd left town to find work, to build a future — for both of them. To escape a world that wouldn't let them be together.

He'd come back too late then.

But not today.

Today, he'd kept his promise.

To honour her. To protect her dignity.

He had seen her. Recognised her in a flash. And created the chaos on purpose — just to run and swap the ticket.

The only thing he didn't know? Her name had changed after marriage.

But had it really? she wondered.

With a lighter heart and a healed soul, she hoisted her younger child onto her hip and holding the hand of the older one firmly, she joined her impatient husband inside the fuming autorickshaw.

CHAPTER TWENTY-ONE

Soap and the Art of Bathroom Levitation

Levitation is an art. All it takes is some soapy water on smooth tiles—or a uniquely intelligent creature—and you too can turn this much-maligned pseudoscientific concept into a practical, if painful, reality.

This morning, mid-air and mid-bath, I had time (and altitude) to reflect on my previous brushes with levitation. None of these attempts were planned, mind you. I've never actively pursued airborne greatness. It's just that the universe seems determined to keep launching me.

The first time was back in college. I was riding my Chetak scooter and made the rookie mistake of following a learner on a moped. We were cruising downhill when he spotted an ice-cream tempo to his left and, like all learners who spot joy, panicked and slammed the brakes.

I slammed into him with all the force my Chetak could muster. He stayed rooted. I, however, took off in a majestic arc over his helmet. In that brief airborne moment, I could see right past the ice-cream tempo... and into the eyes of my dear friend Dnyanesh Talpade, who was behind it, serenely licking an ice cream from bottom to top. Our eyes met mid-lick, mid-flight. The confusion on his face said it all:
Did I just see Rajan fly past, or did they spike the butterscotch?

The next incident was thanks to another intelligent specimen—who cleverly parked his badminton bags at the edge of the court I was playing on. While chasing a particularly flirty shuttlecock, my eyes were skyward, but my foot found the bag. And just like that, I was airborne again, this time across service lines.

To my credit, some training kicked in. I remembered the "how-to-fall" protocol from a long-forgotten PE class. So instead of sprawling, I landed on my shoulder, rolled twice to disperse the impact, and sprang up like a hero—except it probably looked more like a confused octopus trying yoga. I lost the point. And some ego.

The most recent incident happened this very morning—same bathroom, same time (give or take an hour), same mistake. I vigorously soaped up before turning on the shower. It's a proven fact—no surface, not even the holy grail of non-skid tiles, can resist the wrath of still, soapy water. I've tested this theory. Twice.

The first time, I was lucky—close enough to the shower handle to break my fall. But today, I wasn't near anything grab-able. Suspended mid-air like a confused superhero with no superpower, I realized: *I am in a funk.*

I now completely agree with yogis who say the mind is at its clearest while levitating. No mind-altering substance required. I instantly knew what to do. I drew away my left hand—it was already sore from yesterday's ill-advised squash match—leaving my right side to heroically take the brunt.

Gravity, ever reliable, won again. I landed flat on my back. Pain lit up my right wrist, lower back, and shoulder blades in quick succession. Teeth chattered. Bones rattled. And yet—I survived.

Later, I casually narrated the whole episode to my wife with great bravado. She looked alarmed. My long-serving maid of 25 years, however, didn't miss a beat.

"Aaj kuch nahin hoga," she muttered, with veteran nonchalance. "Lekin kal... maha-dard hoga."

Sobering thought, that.

CHAPTER TWENTY-TWO

THE INFINITE PAIN OF GRIEF

Everyone loves chocolates.
But I'm indifferent to them.

And it's not just chocolates I don't care about. It's most things sweet. Colas, *mithai*, toffees...

I was twelve when my sister was diagnosed with diabetes. She was two years older than me.
To me and my eldest sister, who was sixteen then, it meant that Radhika wouldn't be allowed to eat sweets—no chocolates, no sugar, nothing she loved.
That felt terrible, because of the three of us, Radhika was the one most fond of sweets.

My best memories were of us fighting over custard or jelly or chocolates. And now there would be none of that.
Would I eat a chocolate as she watched? Relish that custard while she drank plain, unsweetened milk? Chomp on a pastry while she sat there with nothing?

It wasn't guilt.
It was just... not a good feeling.

That milk chocolate suddenly held no joy—for me, or for Renuka.

Those little pleasures no longer tasted the same.

Back then, getting diabetic chocolates was nearly impossible in India. No Indian company made them, and importing chocolates was illegal. So we'd wait for friends or relatives traveling abroad, hoping they'd bring some back.

For us, it became more important that guests brought diabetic chocolates for Radhika than regular ones for us.

Most didn't know the difference. They'd get "low-cal" chocolates, which was something else altogether. They served no purpose. Those—and regular chocolates—would lie untouched in our fridge for years.

My aunt and uncle (God bless them always), who lived in Italy, were the only ones who truly understood. They'd somehow manage to send diabetic chocolates whenever they found someone traveling to Bombay.

Radhika ate them without much fuss.
I think she was trying not to get attached—perhaps because she didn't know if more would come again.

She'd offer them to us, and we'd eat them and marvel aloud, "It tastes just like regular chocolate!" But it didn't.
Just like how Diet Coke never quite tastes like Coke—these had a tinny sweetness that was nowhere close to the real thing.

That same aunt and uncle also sent artificial sweeteners. My mother would use them to make custard and Indian sweets for Radhika, alongside regular versions for us.

One day, weeks after mom had made custard for us, I was rummaging through the fridge looking for something to eat.
I pulled the lid off a container—and saw a half-eaten bowl of custard made specially for Radhika.

That vessel, untouched for weeks, told me everything: Radhika never really had it.

I'll never forget that moment—the cold draft from the fridge, the chilled stainless-steel bowl, and that frozen-to-ice piece of pink custard.

I never asked for custard after that.

Water soon replaced colas for me.

Even when I moved to a hostel, I never felt the need to drink a soft drink. Ice cream didn't excite me. *Gajar ka halwa* didn't move me. Even trips to Calcutta passed without me craving their legendary sweets.

It wasn't that I hated sweets. I didn't dislike them.

I'd just... grown indifferent.

For most of my teens and twenties, I doubt I ever bought a chocolate or a dessert for myself.

These days, the only time I eat chocolate is when I share it with my wife and son.

And only then do I actually *taste* the sweetness.

The sweetness of sharing. Of togetherness. Of happiness.

It's a feeling I once had. Then lost. Now it's there again.

But it always comes wrapped in a quiet ache.

A pain from somewhere deep inside me.

That throbs and throbs—

And just won't go away.

CHAPTER TWENTY-THREE

PARROT SOUP

Every kid deserves a pet. But if pets could choose, they'd probably vote against this postulate. Let me illustrate with a personal example.

My father, a kindly soul, often found himself torn between the competing demands of his family. On one side were we—the apple(s) of his eye—whom he had clothed, fed, and humored to every limit. And ranged against us was his wife, our mother. The bone of contention? Our undying demand for a pet dog.

Dad knew that all our promises—of walking it, feeding it, even brushing its teeth (yes, I genuinely believed animals brushed their teeth)—were pure doggy poop. He had mentally resigned himself to being the one waking up early to do all the work. But he had no answer to Mom's one non-negotiable: **NO NON-VEG.**

And so, one day, as I was chasing a rubber ball in the compound, I literally collided with Dad as he stepped out of our Fiat, holding a compromise: a **caged parrot**. He confessed how that very afternoon, he and his friend Sundaram had decided to rebel against tradition and each had taken home a parrot for their respective children.

Mom was nonplussed. We were thrilled. Finally, a pet. A vegetarian pet.

Naming him sparked a minor war—mythological, religious, and downright filmi suggestions flew around—but we kids prevailed. He was christened **Chowchow**.

The fellow was docile, moving up and down his cage in quiet dignity. From a Marathi poem at school, we figured he'd love *peru* and *mirchi*, which we generously fed him. We may have overestimated both his appetite and his hygiene preferences, as he proceeded to kick out whatever he didn't eat onto the living room floor. That gave Mom the perfect reason to exile him to the balcony.

That evening, we bragged about our new acquisition to every friend we saw. Soon, there was a queue of kids outside our house that rivaled Jijamata Udyan on a Sunday.

Now Bollywood had painted a very rosy picture of parrots—singing like Tansen, talking like philosophers, and doubling as sidekicks to 70s heroes on bikes. In reality, parrots can just about fly and screech. But not for the crowd of kids, who came armed with flowers, songs, and 70s-style affection—proceeding to scare the feathers off poor Chowchow.

His misery deepened with the winter chill of the balcony until he met his true nemesis: **Kamalabai**.

Mom, being religious, relied on Kamalabai to keep her updated on every *Chaturthi* and *Paurnima*. One look at Chowchow, and Kamalabai's spiritual sensors went into overdrive.

"You haven't bathed him?" she shrieked.
"He's a *Brahmin*, after all!"

Brahmin? A parrot?

We stared at Chowchow more closely. Having recently earned my crossbelt, I imagined a similar ceremony where papa parrot had gifted baby Chowchow his sacred thread. I envied him for having lost it somewhere along the way.

But this reflection was cut short as Kamalabai yanked the cage off the hook and stormed into the bathroom to give Chowchow his first—and last—ritual bath.

Now, the brass taps in our government colony operated at only two speeds: **No Water** and **Niagara Falls**. So forceful was the pressure that we ourselves filled buckets and bathed from them.

Poor Chowchow was subjected to this miniature waterfall. He emerged a feathered mess—soaked, shocked, and clearly traumatized by his unwanted Brahminical initiation. Whatever life was left in him was frozen by the night winds, and two days later, we were devastated to find him lying lifeless in his cage.

His last rites were far from ceremonial—he was quietly buried in some forgotten corner of the colony.

Since then, the very word *pet* has been taboo in our household across generations. In fact, if you examine Aneesha, Vinayak, and Udbhav's baby alphabet books closely, you'll notice the letter **P** stands for many things—but never **pet**.

Epilogue

Mr. Sundaram's parrot took a rather different trajectory.

A timid man himself, Sundaram realized too late that he hadn't brought home a parrot—but a predator. With bloodshot eyes, talons like daggers, and a screech that could split ears, this wasn't a bird—it was a reincarnated hawk.

The day the bird pecked his finger aggressively, Sundaram knew he was doomed.

It soon escaped its cage and established a reign of terror inside the Sundaram household. Things got so bad that the entire family had to lock themselves inside their bathroom one evening and call for help.

This **Garuda-reincarnate** ruled their home for months while they remained caged in their own kitchen. Finally, after several weeks of desperate prayers to the gods that lived above the kitchen shelves, the parrot disdainfully flew away.

But their trauma wasn't over.

The bird often returned to ambush them as they entered or exited the building. Mr. Sundaram, now deeply scarred, developed a pathological aversion to the colour green. Eventually, he hung a framed photo of the parrot among the gods in his kitchen—perhaps to appease it, or maybe just to keep an eye on it.

Part 5

CHAPTER TWENTY-FOUR

PREDATOR

A thick layer of snow permeated even this densest of pine forests. An aerial view would have presented the topography as a stark white picture, punctuated by dark gaps which were the shadows cast by the branches of the trees that dotted the edge of each cluster. A closer inspection would, perhaps for the eagle-eyed, have presented a brief glimmer of a different shade beneath one of the thousand trees. A minute difference in shade for the sharpest of eyes to spot. The observer would magnify that portion several times and attempt in vain to glean what exactly was that shade which seemed so much like the shadows around yet held that sliver of mysterious difference. But all the detailed efforts would reveal nothing and even the keenest of investigators would, with a tired shrug dismiss it for an anomaly of light or a trick of a suspicious mind.

The investigators should indeed have trusted their instincts. For what was captured was indeed unique from the shadows that sulked around. A soul, which had lived all its life in the black shadows of the night. A male with nothing more than the fiercest will to survive and the raw courage to go the extra mile in its pursuit.

For as long as he could remember he'd been alone. From a very early age he'd found himself amidst a pack of slaves carrying their master's load. Inevitably in the lead, searching a way for their survival. The sound of the cracking whip and the cold hunger were his only constant companions. The push for survival meant he developed a sixth sense for danger at a very early age. As he did those powerful muscles and his fierce temper.

Admittedly, he made mistakes and few friends. But his incredible spirit pulled them through the deadliest winters and the most searing of storms. He had forgotten himself, had become lost in his duty. Alone and battered he struggled on in the face of wrathful nature. Then one day, the team slipped through a crack in the ice. All would have been lost but for his efforts. Furiously he broke out and inch by inch clawed out.

The team was broken; bodies lay still. His master left him broken and for dead. But there was breath left in him. Breath enough to fan the fire of life anew. He dragged himself to the warmth and let his broken body heal. Fierce and independent as he was, his instinct was to search for the warmth of collective misery and slavery. But all slaves had their own team leaders, all stupidly unwilling to share their burden.

He scoured the wilderness and found primitive tribes like himself. At first their companionship was pleasant, but soon their despondency irked him and then the day arrived when he broke free from them completely. Ghost-like he covered thousands of miles and quite by accident found her. For someone, unfamiliar to affection, her complete submission was a life-changing moment to him. From that moment, he lived and hunted for her ...and their child. His incredible strength and lightning speed were now marked by stealth and cunning as he pursued deer and stags with infinite patience.

Then one day, as he stood exhausted besides the huge male stag, the wolf pack charged at him. He could have taken two of them, even three perhaps but not all four. Which meant the possibility starvation for his mate and child. So, with tears of rage in his heart he surrendered his kill and found succour in the lonely woods, watching the pack devour what should have been his. The rage moulded itself into a smouldering volcano into which crept the thought of this becoming a regular feature of life.

Distraught he wandered the mountains, desperately making small kills to feed his tiny family. Fear for the first, time gnawed at his heart. He felt his speed falter, his faith in himself seemed to shake. In that desperate condition, he encountered a demon who he thought he'd burnt eons ago. A master.

Sickly, pale and old, the man poured warm milk in a cup. He pointed to his other slaves in chains and to the dull, painfully inadequate fire they shivered before and finally threw at him crumbs of the bread that once was his diet. "Be my slave." The old man whispered, "Hunt and kill for me and you'll have my crumbs..." He reared up in time and went up to the old man and challenged him, "But what are you going to do for us? more than these crumbs? You want me to hunt and kill for you, feed your family and you along with carrying the burden of your slaves! How will you help me? What will you give me?"

The old man recoiled in horror, ""You want equality? You get my chains. That's all I've ever offered."

He struggled with the choice: crumbs for his tiny family, crumbs at least, assured crumbs. On the other hand...

His failures, his anger, his loss to the wolf-pack... all of it came rushing back. He looked at the old man, saw for the first time his wrinkled skin, his red watering crafty eyes and his shaking fingers... He squared his shoulders, looked sadly at the slaves and silently turned and bounded away, disappearing into the blackness which would soon become his alias. For good.

That life, those chains, would never bind him, he thought as he ran soundlessly through the trees. His sense for danger pricked up. Without turning his head, he knew, the leopard was watching him. An idea flashed through his mind, he slowed allowing the big cat to come within a few feet of him and then he ran for his life, inches ahead of the cat. It was touch and go. The wolf-pack was caught completely unawares as they cascaded almost as one atop them. Like greased lightning he slid away as the leopard and the wolf pack slugged it out.

The pack were an equal match for a full-grown male leopard. But just about. For at the end of it, five bodies lay torn and battered in the snow. Soon there would be two more. For he saw the two tiny cubs emerge from the den. They would die in the snow within hours. He walked toward his family without looking back even once. Better them than his own. That was law.

He felt exhilaration, a heady sense of liberation filled him.

The male bison at first took no notice of his inferior adversary. But soon, the efforts of the puny opponent began to irritate, then anger him. The bison was not allowed to drink or eat. Or sleep. Continuously harassed for days sometimes he chased his adversary, who seemed indefatigable. Suddenly he seemed to grow in stature and courage. His attack grew more penetrative, hurt more and more. The bison was bleeding now. Steadily losing strength. His adversary was weakening too, himself being without food or water or sleep but the bison was weakening faster. It was now or never for the bison. One evening as his adversary made his foray, the bison lunged and pushed harder than he usually did and boxed the enemy. In rage he roared and attacked, pinning the smaller body to the ground with his horns. He pressed them into the iron body of his opponent. Their eyes were inches away and the bison looked into the coal-black and fierce eyes of his enemy wanting to see death there.

Instead, there was the fierce energy of life. Baleful and hot. So hot that it seared the bison's courage and broke his attack. He had been tricked! His enemy's teeth sank into his exposed neck and bit out his throat, ripping his gullet out. The bison's last sight was the blood-stained mouth of his killer, watching him in anticipation of his death.

The moon was out full in the cold night sky. His family slept peacefully in the cave behind him. But he was staring restlessly into the night. The winter would end soon. The spring meant his adversary would awaken. The grizzly. They had the same territory. In the many years past, they'd avoided each other. Neither wanting the fight. But this time it would be different. The bear's path would cross his family's and that may happen in his absence.

He would kill the bear. It was that simple. He always understood these simple things. He would kill the bear now, when he wasn't fully rested, his reflexes slower and when he was hungry. It won't be easy, but he would do it. He wasn't young, but he was very, very strong and fierce and far more cunning. He began to draw out his plan.

The bear was awakened not by the winter's chill, but by a peculiar sound. It was nauseating and gut-wrenching. He awoke, very angry and very confused. He rushed out of the cave wanting to destroy that sound that seemed to pull him higher and higher up the mountain.

All the other animals of the forest shivered. Not from the cold but from the sound. For this was the howl of the primordial predator.

The howl of the wolf. And not just any other wolf.

He was the Big, Bad Wolf.

CHAPTER TWENTY-FIVE

MASTER, MASTER, TEACH ME KUNG-FU

This plaintive cry from the boys of our school was heard by our kindly Principal and soon, we were informed that karate classes would be conducted thrice a week at the stage atop the school auditorium. The first-day turnout was humongous and there was barely space to accommodate young boys with dreams in their heads of becoming the next Jackie Chan.

Expecting our instructor to be a meditating Chinese Buddha with a grey beard and a philosophical glint in his eye, we were surprised to see a young Parsee from Charni Road stand in his stead.

Let me spend some time describing this remarkable instructor.

The Parsees are the original Persians, a great race who ruled most of the ancient world for a long period. In the movie *300*, they were wrongly depicted as being effeminate, weak, and poor fighters. Nothing could be further from the truth. The Persians, for most parts of history, had the Greeks properly whupped—including the 300, whom they decimated to a man. Most Indians wouldn't believe this, as Parsees in India, while maintaining their inherent nobility, are law-abiding and peace-loving.

Our instructor was possibly a direct descendant of those fierce warriors who had tamed the Greeks. Of above-average height, a ripped body, with a bearded face in which was enshrined a nose so hooked that an eagle would envy it, and deep-set red eyes which possessed the unique ability of rotating in opposite directions simultaneously.

Above these biological marvels sprouted the bushiest-ever eyebrows any primate ever owned, which met angrily at the very point on his face from where the aquiline nose arose. This warrior was a sight that would have sent shivers down the spine of every Spartan. To match that awe-inspiring look, he had an equally effective, ear-drum-piercing yell—the power of which, we were certain, could dent any shield that stood in his path.

Notwithstanding these natural eliminators, our teacher had an ace up his sleeve. His greatest weapon was actually his mouth. Rather, it was the breath that emanated from it.

The world would never have heard of the great warrior-king Alexander the Great had he ever fought our dear instructor in single combat. For in the course of battle, when these two greats would have been locked in close combat, our instructor would have screeched his breath into the face of he-who-should-have-been-the-conqueror-of-the-world, and the fight would have ended right there.

Had the Americans, who used the gas chamber to carry out capital punishments, ever run out of gas, they would have called our instructor to fill in the role—for a single blast from whose mouth would have done the trick. Such was the noxiousness of the fumes that emerged from him. As if the gas was not enough, it was accompanied by generous amounts of spittle, enough to drown a baby.

The instructor wasted no time with us. He barked for us to begin push-ups. We lazily got down on our palms. Now, our school was the perfect microcosmic model of India when it came to sports and athletics. By this, I mean that sports and athletics were completely absent—not just in our activities but also in our vocabulary.

Did we have a T-shirt for sports day? Yes.
Did we have sports teachers? Yes.
Did we have a PT period? Yes.

But the original objective behind all the above questions and what was being practiced in reality were two separate things. The T-shirt merely added variety to the school uniform. During PT period we played games like saankli, kho-kho, lock & key—which had been abandoned even at district-level competitions.

Mostly we spent the time walking around school and chatting with our portly PT instructors, Mr. Lawrence and Mr. Pingulkar, who were competing against each other to develop a larger paunch. Break time meant we played the same games or football with a stone in our tiny auditorium. The highest form of exercise was during the morning assembly when we had to do Danish exercises.

A viewer from the terrace of the surrounding buildings would have decoded our morning Danish ritual as unique—because he would wonder how so many students could be simultaneously raising their socks or scratching their backs? So insipid was our collective effort.

On some days, our elderly principal would admonish us for our lack of effort. She would look so sad that it would galvanize us to improve our effort microscopically the next day. Our sports day performance could have created records for slowest performances. At inter-school sports events, we rarely won any medal—except at march-past, because we were adept at generally walking around and flailing our empty hands.

So when this instructor yelled for us to begin knuckle push-ups, we characteristically refused and loudly began to complain.

"Thwack, thwak, thwak..." These sounds stunned us! The instructor had, in the span of five seconds, kicked about twenty lazy boys into action. The effect was instantaneous and electrifying!

In unison and without any further time/word-loss, all of us were on our knuckles and heaving our bodies up and down. This was followed by sit-ups and crunches.

"Ech, nee, son, chi..." This is the Japanese numerical count. I never recollected after the number four because pain tended to numb the working of my mind from that point onward.

The effort, though, was driven by the terrifying thought of being stuck with a broken rib, delivered by a resounding, mule-like kick from this ancient warrior—who didn't stop even after what seemed like a thousand counts.

The only other Japanese word I remember is *yamaha*, which meant *stop*! For obvious reasons. Now why would a motorcycle company call itself *stop*? But we couldn't care less if *stop* was *suzuki* or *honda* or *toyota*. It was the sweetest-sounding word for us boys.

The next day we felt like Thakur Baldev Singh from the film *Sholay*, as our hands refused to raise themselves for any purpose.

The next class saw the student attendance fall by 90%. Very soon it was just about 10–15 of us—too middle-class to walk away from a fully paid-up fee. This unfortunately meant that the instructor could keep a closer eye on us. And given that he did not believe in reducing his total kicks per day, it translated into the formula: **higher average kicks per remaining student.**

We had developed some avoidance techniques: roll under the corner cupboard, stand right in front and take the noxious blast from his mouth but avoid the back-bencher-gets-more-kicks approach, etc. All said and done, it was a bruising quarter.

Then the instructor decided to teach us sparring. Our opponent? He, the almighty.

One day he called out, "Who is the strongest among you?"

We all looked toward Nrupal. Now Nrupal was the ideal head-boy material. Tall, strong, athletic, and generous with kids, he'd often ask us to punch him in the stomach to entertain us. Yes, Nrupal was our best bet—the ideal pole-bearer; he'd show this Nazi the mettle of Hill-Grangers.

The instructor asked Nrupal to punch him in the stomach. Nrupal produced a stunning one—it sounded like something Amitabh Bachchan usually delivered. But surprisingly, all it got was loud maniacal laughter from the instructor, whose eyes rotated round and round faster than a merry-go-round.

He then raised his fist and returned a punch to Nrupal's abdomen. It sounded like a nuclear explosion had gone off in his gut. We saw Nrupal's face turn green as he staggered away.

Just as I was measuring the distance between myself and the safety of the closet, I heard him screech my name.

I walked with rubbery legs toward my demise. I felt instant sympathy for all men who had ever been executed.

Survival wrote a plan in my head: *"Drop. Faint before his fist hits you."*

Now I was standing in front of him. The full blast of his breath hit me as he screamed at me to strike him. The breath numbed me. I felt my hand move forward weakly in the form of a blow that wouldn't have tickled a baby.

He screeched in scornful laughter and told me to try again. More poisonous fumes hit me. My head was swimming as I attempted a weaker second. Then I saw his fist hit me.

I felt now as though the Pokhran bomb had fallen on me. I waited for gravity to pull me down. But to my horror, I realized that all the laws of physics had betrayed me in my moment of need—except one: the centrifugal force. It was solely acting on me, defiantly keeping me standing on my papery legs, to my utter despair.

The instructor couldn't believe his red, swirling eyes. I saw the next punch approach me in slow motion... soon followed by darkness, my old friend.

Many years later, I was in college and walking by Charni Road when, near the footbridge, I saw a familiar sight approaching me. It was the instructor.

Our eyes met. His swirled. I looked around and saw a BEST bus passing by. I jumped into it and didn't get down till it reached its very last stop.

CHAPTER TWENTY-SIX

UNMENDABLE

She's broken. And the pieces lie scattered.
If she was cheap, would it have mattered?
Maybe she was rare. Perhaps, precious—
Held flowers with fragrance delicious.
    Maybe she marked an occasion—
A wedding, a birth, a celebration.
Bright and translucent,
She looked magnificent.
Paid for, or worth her weight in gold,
Carrying memories seldom retold.
    She was once happy.
To someone, she meant plenty.
Too soon, she made plans—
To live, to laugh, to dream a lifespan.
    A ruthless ball—or was it a word?—
Flew in through the window of her world.
Unerring fate struck at her heart.
She wobbled. And fell apart.
    No gum, no glue, no technology
Can mend her. How hollow the apology.
A tear for a faithful companion—
Find peace in the calm of the ocean.

CHAPTER TWENTY-SEVEN

THE LOST YEARS

When did I lose that race? Long before I even began running it. Looking back, I wonder if I even ran it at all. I was the proverbial mass of 'the others', I guess. The problem always begins when you don't listen to yourself. When you're accommodating and trying to do what others are doing—or what others want you to do.

On the other hand, to be fair, maybe expecting a 15-year-old to know what he wants is asking a bit too much...

Looking back at the environment I was in, I can sympathize with that 15-year-old and maybe understand his pressures. I was surrounded by academic scholars in my family. Every relative I had was breaking new academic ground.

"CA at only 20 years!"

"MTech from IIT!"

"Top US University!"

"IBM employee!"

And then, the despairing commentary about the few who weren't up to the mark:

"CA only on the second attempt, pah!"

"Ordinary engineering college—not IIT!"

"Got into only dentistry... couldn't get MBBS."

"Failed his BA!"

I'd feel tremendously sorry for these kin. They were nice guys, you know—actually more fun to be with. Unlike the academic scholars who'd speak to me in monotonic syllables and quiz me on every conceivable topic during the few minutes I was around them, these so-called 'failures' had stories to tell—who in the neighbourhood had run away with whom, which marriage was breaking down, or some dirty jokes. Better still, they'd pull me along for an adult movie or a trek in the forest adjoining Mumbai. But disapproving frowns from elders would follow, and regretfully, I'd break away from them and return to the drudgery of monotones and tests.

Marriages, thread ceremonies, births or deaths—after the initial small talk, all conversations would inevitably veer toward us kids and our academic progress. And I knew, with a sinking heart, that my turn was coming.
I was in Class XI or XII. My moment of reckoning had arrived.
They were all eagerly awaiting my performance—and soon I would be dissected, then either put on a pedestal or thrown to the dogs.

So there I was—a science student, without any love for the subject, with only a desperate desire to do well and not be classified as a 'failure', trying to match up with the few million of my age. I tried hard—got into a good college, a good coaching institute, took tuitions in French and other scoring subjects, studied sincerely, attended all classes, gave up games, movies, TV... but my heart simply wasn't in it.

Out from seven in the morning with only short breaks in between, I'd return home by about ten at night. Exhausted. Mother would have food hot and ready.

Father would quietly cut fruits to save me the trouble.

He'd lost his own father early, seen poverty as a child, and fought his way to becoming a university topper. A highly respected man, he never forced me into anything.

My sisters would switch off the TV, their only source of entertainment, so as not to distract me.

My throat would choke. I'd feel guilty for not trying harder.

I was lonely. And growing lonelier by the day.

My classmates and immediate friends were immersed in the theories of light, sound, ellipses, and limits. Every conversation was about how many times they'd revised the portion, how last year's batch performed, the latest IIT paper, the 'practs', and how electronics students got 5% extra, so their maximum marks could now go up to 105%.

One hundred and five percent! God, give me a break. Was this even real?

You know, they weren't bad or mean at all. They were good people. They meant well. Just that there was now a gulf between us, and it was widening every day.

Maybe I should have called out to them.

I know they would've understood and helped me.

But for some residual mix of pride and inertia, I remained silent—and drifted even farther away.

At the bus stop, it was physics.

On the bus, some obscure question that had cropped up 15 years back in an old paper.

In college, it was all portions, topics, revisions.

And then the classes. Agroos. Ideal for Scholars.

In a brightly lit, freezing room, sixty of us sat cramped together, trying to outdo each other as if we were prisoners planning a jailbreak.

The crowd here was from suburban colleges—tougher, more competitive.

Conversations hovered around obscure areas with the remotest chance of appearing in any exam, but raised only to signal superior preparation and discourage the rest.

It worked. It crushed me.

Often, the *batata wada* or *bhajiya* I'd just bought from Messer's D. Damodhar Mithaiwala to quell my demonic hunger would turn tasteless and unappetizing. Fit only to be handed to some bemused beggar.

The only part of the day I enjoyed was the bus ride. I'd always take the double-decker and sit right in front by the window. The cool breeze, the busy streets—they offered a welcome diversion.

The hawker at the corner.

The worried-looking girl crossing the road.

Even the rather fattish cop—his expanding middle carried a story.

But in 20 minutes, the diversion would end. And I'd be back in my programmed world.

Of course, there were times I'd chuck it all and join my friends for a fantastic game of football in the rain or gully cricket. But it always took just one question from some passing uncle or 'well-wisher'—

"Aren't you in 12th? Looks like you're fully prepared."

Those words hurt more than a football to the gut.

And shame-faced, I'd retreat—never to be seen again for months.

I needed some escape. So I'd rise early and jog at the racecourse—even during the rains.

I'd find peace in the stillness of morning and the gentle patter of rain.

Its wetness was comforting.

I must have cut a strange sight to the startled horses and stray dogs—a lone figure plodding through darkness and drizzle.

And then, month after month, the postman would ring and drop another guilt bomb—The Brilliant Tutorial IIT course set. A fresh, crisp set of notes, tests, and analyses. I never had the courage to open more than one. I remember opening the first. What I read horrified me. I couldn't comprehend even the first sentence.

Was this maths? Physics? Chemistry?

"Nooooo," something inside me screamed.

I shoved it back in.

What I don't know can't hurt me, I thought.

Neatly, I arranged them in the bottom of my cupboard—some still unopened in their brown packets.

Occasionally, while placing a fresh one, I'd feel a twinge of regret.

But numbness had begun to settle in.

One night, long after everyone had fallen asleep, I gave up after a frustrating battle with inorganic chemistry. I paced the room and opened the cupboard I shared with my sisters.

There, neatly stacked on her shelf like my tutorials, were her English Literature books.

Only, they weren't textbooks. They were the works of the world's greatest writers—whom, of course, I had no clue about.

I picked the thinnest one—*Leaves of Grass* by Walt Whitman.

I turned the page.

"Come said my soul, such verses for my body let us write..."

I didn't understand it. But something in it moved me.

I returned to my table, put aside inorganic chemistry—and began to read.

The morning felt brighter.

There was now something to look forward to.

My family was taken aback by my sudden burst of late-night energy.

They must've seen it as a good sign.

In reality, it was the opposite.

Still, night after night, my tryst with great minds continued.

Sometimes an American family struggling through the Great Depression.

Sometimes the expectations of young Pip.

A guilt-ridden pilgrim's progress.

A boy from Malgudi.

A satirical Irishman mocking British society.

I was enthralled. Gripped.

I'd found a different world—a world I could understand, enjoy, belong to.

To those great men, I remain eternally grateful—for giving expression and vividness to a lonely, suffering 16-year-old boy.

Of course, time passed. Exams came. Some more exams. And then more.

In between were my sister's exams, too.

One morning, as we were both getting ready, she muttered: "God, I haven't read *Great Expectations* and there's bound to be a question on it!"

I felt for her.

Being in the same boat for much of my syllabus, I said, "The key bit is Pip's realization of his benefactor—and how it changes his idea of success."

She turned, stunned. I explained whatever I had understood.

I'll never forget her expression.

She quickly recovered, "As long as I pass!"

I wished I could say the same. But that would've been suicidal.

I floated through exams. I have only hazy recollections. And then, they were over.

Except for the IIT-JEE.

In the month between boards and JEE, regret prompted me to dust and rearrange the Brilliant Tutorials material. I wouldn't need it anymore.

That exam was memorable—it was the first exam where I fell asleep.

And it was a deep, comforting sleep.

The professor shook his head in disapproval.

My only consolation: I'd tried hard on the English paper.

My dear father, heartbroken for his struggling son, took us on a beautiful vacation to Kashmir.

Two years of tension melted like the snow at Pahalgam.

Colour returned to my cheeks.

Until the results.

"I paaaaassseddd!" my sister squealed.

I could only offer a wan smile.

When my result came, my dear friend Raju walked silently with me down Marine Drive.

He'd done well. But he didn't show it.

My parents said nothing. That made it harder.

Then the JEE results came.

My friends headed to Powai.

My mother asked, "Don't you..."

One look at my face, and she stopped.

My father quietly took my marksheet and applied to colleges.

"Come on," he said, "Let's try."

Sometimes, I wished he'd just yelled at me.

But he never has—not then, not ever.

Then one day, he came to me.

"See, I told you! You're not as bad as you think. You've got admission in an engineering college—it's a bit far... in Manipal. But it's a good one."

"Manipal?" I asked.

I shrugged. Looked at him.

"If it makes him happy," I thought, "I'll go."

MIT Manipal. But that's another story.

My son,

You may wonder why I'm writing this now.

I want you to understand—it doesn't matter. Success, failure—they don't matter. Life matters.

There will be ups and downs. That's part of the game.

But life must be lived. And enjoyed.

Speak your mind. Do what you want. Don't think too hard.

You're way too young to have it all figured out.

And I never want any pressure to wipe that cheerful smile off your face.

You'll do just fine in life.

And I'm already proud of you. So proud that you don't need to do anything more to earn it.

I only want to see you smile—because that tells me you're living your life, having a good time.

That's all I've ever wanted since the magical moment I first held you in my arms.

FINAL SALUTE

The soldier walked alone under the baking mid-morning sun. His train had pulled into the dusty, elevated platform that twenty-odd villages called a railway station. The district itself was just a statistic—a number in a ledger, devoid of faces, names, or voices. No one in the echelons of power bothered to put flesh, blood, and bone to it. Livestock, humans, people—all flattened into numbers that made up this vast, timeless nation.

He had expected to be received by family and friends. It had been five years since he left from that very platform, lovingly placed on the train by a packed crowd of villagers, proud of their valiant son who carried the pride and lineage of their community. He was their symbol of courage in a war that had suddenly rocked the country.

They'd showered him with blessings, extracting promises that he would make a name for himself and bring honour to their people.

The measly salary of a soldier was a fortune in a land racked by drought and famine. Families had sons to spare but not food for mouths. A soldier on the front was a matter of pride. It was as though *they* were at war, risking *their* lives, when in fact all they did was lie back on their cots, drawing on their hookahs, taking credit for the young man's toil.

His father had been the proudest man in the village that day. His brothers, lions. His friends had tears in their eyes and assured him that his family was safe in their care. Some eyes flickered with jealousy, hidden behind smiles and slaps on the back. But the young man, generous as he was brave, acknowledged their praise and their bitterness with a ready, warm smile.

In all the din, though, he looked out for one special person. His eyes searched the crowd. And just as the train began to pull away, he caught sight of her—blushing, standing under the dried tree at the mouth of the platform. Her face was veiled, but her eyes sparkled with a thousand promises. Promises she'd whispered each time they met for a few stolen minutes behind the ancient ruins.

Only his dog seemed unhappy at his parting, howling and circling between his legs as if to hold him back.

Five years of war.

As nations used the lifeblood of their youth to score meaningless points, the real reasons blurred. Objectives faded. The deaths of thousands were quietly buried as "casualties" on the inner pages of newspapers.

The war-mongering that once fired up the populace slowly waned as the country grew confused at the meandering conflict, the stalemates, the lack of progress. Enthusiasm turned to apathy. Apathy was replaced by forgetting, as the real and immediate issues of food and survival took centre stage.

Through it all, the soldier wrote home. Letters from the front, full of courage, longing, hope. At first he received warm replies. Then worried ones. Then notes that mirrored the nation's mood. And finally, none at all.

He bore no grudge. He understood their pain. He even believed that for all the blood and fear, his life was clearer—his purpose, at least, was known. Unlike those who woke up wondering whether there would be food on the table that day.

With this in mind, he fought harder. Braver. With more purpose. He earned a reputation among the enemy.

Strangely, he never felt hatred for the enemy across the fence. When he thought of them, he only saw himself—another young man, worried, responsible, unwilling to die.

Now, he was returning. Discharged with honours. Unfit for duty.

His duty had placed him in the line of a sudden enemy attack. But being the simple man he was, he didn't run. He stayed at his post. Even after the boiling machine gun jammed. He attacked the oncoming tank with his bayonet, some stones, and sheer will. His bravery galvanised his fleeing regiment. They rallied. Together, they turned the tide in what would be etched in history books as one of the bravest battles ever fought.

They took the honours that night—even as the enemy tank took his leg.

A wooden leg dragged behind him as he made his way to his village. His round haversack rested on his back.

He wondered why the station had been empty. He'd sent a telegram. Perhaps it never reached. Or maybe they had received it—and didn't know how to face him. He held no blame. He was eager to meet them. Eager to restart life.

He grinned as he picked up pace. The sun was relentless, but the soldier met it with a challenge in his eyes.

It wasn't yet evening when he entered the village.

The headman and elders were seated beneath the great banyan that marked the village centre. He greeted them.

They looked at him... then looked away. A brief nod. A puff on a hookah. Conversation resumed. As though he were just another strand of the tree. Not meriting much.

He moved on.

Friends were busy. Some took time to place him. When they did, pity jumped into their eyes. He was not used to pity. And so, once he felt his smile being stretched, he left.

He hurried to his home. The welcome was lukewarm.

His father's eyes, once shining with pride, now held questions about his usefulness to a hand-to-mouth household. His brothers' eyes held calculations—how to keep what had been his share of the land.

The soldier faced this moment like he had faced the tank. Calm, direct, honourable.

He told his father he would not stay. He assured his brothers that he claimed no right to land he had not tilled. He refused everything but a glass of water.

Then he walked to the ancient ruins.

They were empty.

And so, too, were the promises that had once sparkled in a pair of veiled eyes.

For once, his warm smile slipped. His face—strong, though not handsome—showed a flicker of wistfulness. His great big heart, for that infinitesimal second, missed a beat.

Even the father of all life seemed to acknowledge the moment, softening the late evening light that stoked his bent head.

A warm, moist nudge pressed into his palm.

He turned.

His dog looked up at him.

He hadn't been greeted by voices, but this—this was loyalty without language.

A moment later, he was flung to the earth by the sheer exuberance of the animal's joy.

Warmth and life surged back into his sinewy frame. He got back on his feet, slung the haversack onto his sweat-streaked shoulder, and with a grin and a whistle, stepped back onto the road to *wherever*.

His dog followed, happily at his feet.

True soldiers fight on many horizons.

Part 6

CHAPTER TWENTY-NINE

NO APPLICATION FOR OLD MEN

"Rajan, what is this?"

My 82-year-old father was holding out a newspaper insert from a food delivery app promising a free samosa and lassi combo from a famous halwai nearby.

"Appa, this is a mobile app that delivers food from eateries in the vicinity."

"That's okay," he said, squinting at the leaflet. "But where's the telephone number I can call to get this free offer?"

I explained, as patiently as I could, "Appa, there's no number. You have to download the app on your smartphone and order through it to avail the offer."

Appa had always refused to keep a smartphone. The screen was too tiny for him to read anything, and the endless stream of WhatsApp jokes had left him completely exasperated.

"So you're telling me I can't avail of this offer just because I don't have a smartphone? I can't believe this. In India, how many people have smartphones? Most people have simple phones like mine. So we're unwanted, is it?

Wait, let me call the halwai. He'll give it to me directly."

Of course, that didn't happen.

A much chagrined Appa returned from the call, shaking his head in disbelief. "He says the offer isn't from him but from the app people — and they pay him full price! That would cost a lot! Why do they want to feed wealthy people for free and not give it to poor people without smartphones?"

Time to break it to him gently.

"Appa, this company is giving an introductory offer to its target audience — to get them on the app, make them use it frequently, build a habit, and eventually acquire them as lifetime customers."

He looked at me, baffled. "But that must take years! How do they make money or pay salaries in the meantime?"

"They don't. Not right away, anyway. They get money from investors — PE firms, VCs, seed funds, angel investors — who pour in millions of dollars."

Appa stared at me for a moment and then said, "I don't get it. These investors pay delivery companies to make huge losses, but won't give that money to actual restaurants and hotels that are already running? And all this just because people are getting too lazy to walk down the street for a meal? Not because they want better food?"

"I'm not sure what their full plan is, Appa. But yes, the belief is that these companies are the future."

A pause. Then I offered, "Should I order you a samosa and lassi anyway?"

"Forget it! I asked for it because it was free. Otherwise, who wants to eat that halwai's stale samosa?"

CHAPTER THIRTY

ENEMY

There's one person I consider to be my enemy. He's this little boy who lives close by. He has this incredible way of ruining everything that I painstakingly build. Take the other day for instance, I was walking out of my apartment having to explain a particularly sticky issue to my boss, when he suddenly slammed into me from nowhere! Screaming and hollering, he ruined the moment so completely that from that day on, my relationship with my boss was irreparably damaged.

Another time, I was in the middle of a function at home; innumerable guests to handle and food to be served when my daughter accidentally dropped her food on the boy. Oh, the ruckus he created! The poor girl was terribly distraught and so was my wife. The guests looked at each other in bewilderment as though asking, "Where did this ill-mannered boy suddenly appear from?"

Mischievous, rude and thoroughly self-centered, he always makes his appearance just at the moments when I'm most vulnerable. He enjoys cracking mean jokes at the expense of others, laughs at the sight of harmless animals wailing in fear, is petulant when he's refused, throws tantrums for small things and at the first available opportunity, he passes on his work to others. He refuses to grow up or to change.

It's been many years now and it's with great difficulty that I've learnt to control him. It began with me accepting his existence and acknowledging that unless I control him first in a situation, he will run riot and ruin everything. Subduing him has been among my greatest achievements, for after that is when I have truly discovered myself and what I can be.

Unfortunately, we don't get to choose our enemies. Sometimes we're born with them. And some of our enemies are a part of our lives. Like this little boy who lives inside my head.

CHAPTER THIRTY-ONE

PURI BAAT

Sports are about specialization. Very few athletes play more than one sport. Some even specialize in just one form of a single sport. And worldwide, experts and commentators too tend to focus only on sports they know well. Many of the great ones have even been champions themselves.

But Doordarshan in the 1980s, being the accidental trailblazer it was, decided — in its infinite wisdom — to hand over the entire genre of sports coverage to a single specialist: Dr. Purshottam Suri.

Now, a minor technicality nobody bothered checking — Dr. Suri hadn't earned a doctorate in sports commentary. He was, in fact, a dentist.

Let's not delve into the 'strategy' behind this decision. It's enough to note that a country of nearly-a-billion people with not a single Olympic medal to its name was saddled with a dentist who served as sports commentator, expert analyst, quizmaster, judge, jury, executioner, Olympics rep, news capsule presenter, and self-declared sports guru.

Dr. Suri may have been a good, bad, mediocre, or downright dangerous dentist — we'll never know. But perhaps when you spend your life in a room with a companion who lies there, mouth wide open, capable only of gargling noises, with a drill whirring as background music, and your own face masked... you begin to thirst for human conversation. Even if it's just your own.

And boy, did Dr. Suri love the sound of his own voice. For someone who likely hadn't played a single sport — not even ludo — he had somehow amassed an encyclopaedic knowledge of every human sport, including, I suspect, extinct ones. It gave him the perfect excuse to host every sports program and every conceivable quiz that aired on DD.

So whether it was Wimbledon, the Cricket World Cup, or the FIFA finals, it was Dr. Suri's morose, unexciting face that greeted us, mouthing off his "expert opinion." His oral stamina matched only by his encyclopaedic rambling, it was usually well past the first Indian wicket, the first goal, or even the first set, by the time we got to see any actual live action.

To make things worse, DD had a habit of interrupting thrilling sports action with a news bulletin delivered by anchors who had clearly never experienced orgasms in their lives. Dr. Suri would then serve as the awkward interface between an electric match and an expressionless newsreader, teaching an entire generation of young Indians the virtue of patience.

Sometimes we'd return from this interruption just in time for the prize distribution ceremony.

To his credit, Dr. Suri was a saviour when the live signal snapped. This was India of the '80s, remember — not the economic powerhouse it's now convinced the world it is. Live broadcasts were choppy and unreliable. But every time the screen froze or the feed cut out, there he was: Dr. Suri, solemn as ever, providing "deep insights" into the twists and turns of a game we weren't actually watching. Nobody remembers a single sentence he ever said, but all of us remember that tireless jaw, that unblinking eye, and the sense that even Duracell bunnies envied his stamina.

As DD evolved, it entered the quiz scene. Siddhartha Basu's *Quiz Time* became a nationwide hit — it was sharp, modern, and had schoolkids from across the country participating.

Not to be left behind, Dr. Suri launched his own sports quiz show.

Hosted, of course, by... himself.

Two things stood out. One, his wardrobe was trapped in the 1970s — bell-bottoms and tight polyester tee-shirts. And two, he was the most stingy, joyless quizmaster ever known to humankind.

In what seemed like a direct competition with *Quiz Time*, Dr. Suri too featured schoolchildren — only to proceed to crush their spirits. His questions could stump the very record-holders they were based on. He seemed to take sadistic pleasure in digging up obscure facts from the deepest corners of sports trivia. The show featured two sounds: Dr. Suri's voice, and the buzzer.

Once — just once — a bespectacled, nervous kid managed to get an answer right. Dr. Suri looked stunned. But he wasn't giving up that scratchy tee-shirt prize so easily. He immediately asked a follow-up question to "complete the answer." The poor kid floundered.

Triumphant, Dr. Suri reached to pull back the tee-shirt when he noticed the audience was on the verge of mutiny. Reluctantly, he handed over the prize with a muttered comment:

"I hope this tee-shirt is one size small for you because your answer was only partially right."

Why am I dredging up this ghost from our Doordarshan-haunted past?

Because the other day, while flipping channels to catch the Olympics, I landed on DD Sports. And there he was. The voice, a bit trembly now. The co-commentators, still struggling to get a word in. The acrylic tee-shirt, bell bottoms — still there. The same inability to shut up.

Dr. Purshottam Suri.

Alive, unblinking, jaw moving, and still going on and on.

CHAPTER THIRTY-TWO

FAILURE FATHER

It's not easy to reconcile to a fate where your father is a disappointment to you. I never had much in life, we never had much in life. We went to second class schools, lived in a cramped house in a distant suburb, where wires hung on the inside and water and moss seeped on the out.

My father was a nobody. He worked as no one in particular at an office that was nothing in particular. Then the office shut down and he was jobless for some time and then would find an occasional job. Somehow, he kept doing such odd jobs in between being unemployed.

We had food and cheap adequate clothes. Everything in life was a tight fit. Just paid our fees in time. Just had enough in the wallet to get home. Just had enough balance in the phone to be active. Just had enough space at home to fit us all in it.

While I never said anything about my disappointments to my father, I never hid my feelings either. I was quite vocal about the opportunities my friends had or the kind of phones they used and the bikes they rode. Father would listen quietly and say nothing. Mother would divert the topic.

It always surprised me to know that theirs was a love marriage. Because neither of them spoke about it or behaved as if it was one.

Father did his odd jobs and returned usually late. Mother was so busy the whole day, she hadn't a moment to talk to us. But on some occasions when we'd sit together as a family or when a relative of friend would pop by, the talk would reoccur.

Then there was one thing, more like dad's ritual. He'd make a painting of mom, once a year. Not on any particular day, but just like that. It wasn't that he would begin on her birthday or anniversary or anything like that. Mom would be telling him to paint, because he had once been a promising artist and then everyone would forget about it. Days, weeks, months would go by and then voila, we see that either dad would be painting or he'd have finished painting.

It was always the same painting.

Of mother's.

Some years they would be in colour, some years in charcoal. Sometimes they were surprisingly candid, other times a portrait. They captured her well. Her frowns of worry that had become permanent of late. The grey in her hair, initially at front, then her sides and finally almost everywhere. The softness in her gaze, the sweat of her brow, the unkemptness of her clothes, the half-smile in her eyes.

My father's brush did her full justice.

It was nice to put up as my WhatsApp status on Mother's Day or some occasion like that, as a story on Instagram or send it to some girls in my class to get some hearts and likes.

Sometimes we would make a show of it as a reel; Dress up in our finest and ask dad to give one to mom on her birthday and the rest of us would clap our hands and sing 'Happy Birthday'. Dad would say nothing, look down on the floor and smile and mom would also smile but worriedly so. We'd all tell Dad that his painting is great on camera and ask him to paint more.

He'd say nothing just turn away. We'd then turn to mom who'd weakly protest saying that nothing would make her happier than if he could turn into a profession, especially one that paid them better. Then she'd mutter something and dive back into the world of her tiny kitchen.

One day, during one such celebration, dad's school friend, told us how dad had been a promising artist in school, but ever since he met mother in college, he has only been painting her. If his brush touched the canvas, it would automatically draw/sketch/paint her. It was like he could only paint her.

"She'd become like a stuck record in his head, hahaha" his friend laughed.

Dad looked down, shook his head and muttered, "Chod na yaar, kya purnai baat yaad kar raha hai..."

Then everyone would crack jokes at Dad and mom's expense, and the party would end.

"Hussain ne Madhuri ko banaya Gajagamini aur Baba ne aai ko banaya Gajamummy! Hehehe" (Hussain made Madhuri 'Gajagamini' Dad makes mom 'Gajamummy')

Come the next year, and again Dad would unfailingly paint another picture of mom.

Even mom would get irritated by them, occasionally.

"Kaye me punah?" (What me again?)

And the jokes would do the rounds again

"Kaye auntie? Alia Bhatt ka karega toh ghar bhi nahi bachega!" (If he draws Alia Bhatt, he won't even have a home)

So it went on. Year after year.

Then one day, finally the heart of my failure father, failed him forever.

He had left nothing for us, except a trunk full of paintings of mother. To make matters worse, that very day we were handed an eviction notice from the municipal authorities since our entire apartment block had become weak and dilapidated and a hazard for its tenants.

Furious with my father for leaving us in such a condition, I took the trunk full of his paintings and flung them out of our tiny balcony onto the expressway that lay past the crumbled boundary walls.

Scores of those paintings, each with mother's image fluttered and floated all over the busy expressway. All the cars came to a grinding halt as the papers and canvases cascaded over both sides of the expressway. Drivers and occupants came rushing out of their cars angrily.

Then something strange happened.

They caught sight of the paintings floating by, some stuck on their cars and windshields and everyone registered the contents.

They were all the paintings of the same woman, albeit across her lifetime.

And an incredible thing began happening.

Everyone on the road began taking picture of those paintings! Some took videos, others put it in their feeds, some went live, others began broadcasting it.

The lifetime of a housewife.

Her freshness, expectations, love, joys, hopes, aspirations, realities, worries, concerns, moments, anxieties, festivities, celebrations, events, days, sadnesses. Her life, caught on canvas, with such depth, intensity and profundity. It was as though her soul was speaking through those images.

Even the greatest of artists of the world, couldn't have captured the depth of her feeling, across a life span, like this. These weren't drawn, they'd been created, molded by both, the artist and the muse, together. If she'd bared her all to him, then he too could see nothing but her.

It was all there, floating in the cosmos, reminiscent of a classical era movie. Beautiful because it can never be recreated.

I got many calls that night. My mother's paintings had gone viral.

Finally, we had an offer from an art collector.

"Individually they're worth nothing." He said, in all honesty, "but together, one after the other, like that?" he blew a kiss.

Mother was sitting quietly in her corner and weeping.

"I'm sorry." I heard myself say, "But these are not for sale."

CHAPTER THIRTY-THREE

SHAMELESS

The unlucky ones got to live in Mongolia. Which, in MIT back in those days, meant Blocks D9 and D10.

Mongolia — because their entrances opened into the gutters of the Cosmo mess. Because it was a forgotten corner of the hostel campus. Because in hot, sweaty April afternoons or stormy July mornings, the walk to class felt like a trek across continents.

Because nobody really lived there — except ghosts, strays, and the unfortunate few of us who had to explain, twice, where exactly we were holed up.

The only other species who shared space with us in this MITian Mongolia was the Great Indian Pariah.

Hold on, that's no rare toad or exotic bird. Just the very common mongrel. *Gully ka kutta*. Local dog. Plural, actually. Packs of them. Drawn to the Cosmo kitchen's generous flushing of bones into the open gutter that choked and spluttered just outside our block.

They'd gather like clockwork, howl, fight, and throw their nightly orgies right around the time the human body is biologically designed to shut shop.

But being adjustable Indians, we adjusted. We let the occasional dog crash indoors during heavy rain or heat.

And to their credit, most of them knew not to overstay the welcome.

Until *he* arrived.

Shameless.

Now before we meet this uniquely revolting specimen of *Canis lupus familiaris*, let me introduce you to my good friend and fellow Mongolian — JP.

JP is among the friendliest humans to have walked this earth. Most MITians would vouch that he was also the most popular person in our batch.

He bore no malice, harboured no grudges. Always ready with a kind word and a readier shoulder, JP was our campus's resident Good Samaritan.

Such was the affection we had for him that we all ignored his one tragic flaw: a legendarily poor aim.

Try as he might, he couldn't hit the broad side of a hostel wall. Even at his best, his missiles would miss by a foot; at his worst, by kilometers. But JP never let that dent his spirit.

On walks back from college or TC, he'd casually lob stones at random targets while chatting with us. We never mocked the misses. There just weren't any hits to celebrate.

And this gentle soul, this universal friend of man and beast — took singular offence to one creature alone: Shameless.

We all hated Shameless. He earned the name. He was eminently dislikeable and thoroughly hateable.

Shameless, to put it politely, was the Lance Armstrong of the Cosmo bone pack.

No, he wasn't a dopehead or a doghlete.

He just had no testicles.

Since no one performs testicle extractions on street dogs, we assumed he was born that way. Yet, despite lacking the equipment, he had the bearing of a pimp.

And like his human counterparts, he derived his pleasures not from the act, but from orchestrating it. Shameless took a perverse joy in lining up members of his pack — male and female — for loud, public displays of affection right outside our block.

We tried to look the other way. Perhaps, we told ourselves, he was just compensating — poor sod. But then he crossed the line.

He moved in.

At first, he curled up near our door. Then, seeing no resistance, he parked himself at the entrance. Soon, he sprawled in the passage. Finally, he made the square behind our rooms — where the bathrooms were — his personal den.

We tried nudging him out. He didn't flinch. Shouted at him. Nothing.

It became a daily irritation — to return from the blistering sun carrying an unmanageable drawing board or to trudge in, drenched by the rain, only to find Mr. Shameless spread-eagled in our already miserable quarters.

Dirt, stink, and gutter juice in tow.

We never really figured out what *exactly* about Shameless triggered JP, but it was clear something did.

JP — who'd help a lizard cross the corridor — would erupt with rage at the mere sight of Shameless. He led the war effort against him with unmatched passion.

Unfortunately, his lifelong handicap — the aim — was a major liability in any war.

Time and again, he'd corner Shameless, only for his stone to land meekly meters away, allowing the mutt to trot off with a mocking glance over his shoulder.

Every miss only fuelled JP's resolve. He turned creative

— mugs of water kept handy, buckets filled in advance, strategic sneak attacks plotted by torchlight.

But Shameless was persistent. Like a bad coin, he kept turning up. And with every return, he grew more stubborn. And JP? More deranged.

He developed a sixth sense for Shameless's entry. He could sniff it. Leap from sleep. Spring into action.

It all came to a head one lazy, hot afternoon.

Shameless had sneaked in again and was snoring away peacefully in the backyard. JP roused me. We shut the door that connected the passage to the yard.

There he was — curled up in the corner, oblivious to the plot unfolding inside.

We quietly filled an iron bucket in the bathroom. But the sloshing water must've tipped off Shameless. He opened one eye and spotted us.

Realising the door was shut and his exit routes limited, he began inching toward the one possible escape — a tiny hole at the base of the yard wall, meant for flood water drainage.

What followed was a scene of high drama and low dignity.

We were racing the clock — or rather, the flow of water versus the crawl of a canine Houdini.

Seeing the odds turning, JP didn't wait for the bucket to fill. With a cry that came from the depths of his exhausted soul, he hurled the water — and accidentally, the bucket — at Shameless.

The water hit him square on the butt.

The bucket, too, followed in perfect synchrony. It struck his wet rear with a loud clang and sent him sliding through the hole like a lubricated torpedo.

Physics was on full display. Kinetic energy of the bucket transferred to Shameless's backside, turning him into a projectile of disgust.

It was beautiful.

We ran out around the block to witness the aftermath — perhaps a limping Shameless, yelping in defeat.

Instead, there he was — 200 meters away — at the edge of the hockey field, trotting happily, no worse for wear. He turned, looked back, and with his usual flourish, began licking his privates.

That was it. The final insult.

JP, beyond himself, picked up the nearest rock. And for once — for the first and perhaps only time in his life — he launched it straight and true.

Some memories are etched forever.

The brilliant blue sky. The red dust of the hockey field. The brown wall beyond it. Shameless, victorious, basking in his perverse glory. And JP's rock, flying like a divine missile, guided by destiny — or sheer, righteous rage.

We never saw Shameless again.

That stone, which spent a lifetime in the sky, came down unerringly — right on the one spot on Shameless's body where there ought to have been two balls... but weren't.

CHAPTER THIRTY-FOUR

HAPPY ENDINGS

I woke up suddenly to the feeling that something was not right. The house was unusually busy for a Sunday morning. My exhausted mind picked up the sound of heavy grinding, above which roared the excited whirr of the mixer, interspersed with the crackling of hot oil deep-frying potato bondas.

The house comprised Dad, Mom, and me. Both Dad and I were well-trained men—we never asked for anything special to be cooked. We gobbled up whatever Mom dished out, wiping our plates clean. Not that we desired anything—Mom was a great cook, and none of us were foodies. So why all this heavy-duty cooking on a Sunday?

Guests.

And not just any guests—some real, real important ones to warrant all this effort. Moreover, these were outsiders. If they'd been relatives, the cooking would've been casual. Our relatives too, well trained by their respective spouses, would simply eat whatever was served, without a word.

Still wiping the sleep from my eyes, I was startled to see Mom seated at the foot of my bed.

This was rare.

In our rather orthodox home, I was a bit of a pariah—the meat-eating, poonal-losing, sandhyavandanam-forgetting, late-rising, non-Tamil speaking, non-first-ranking, non-banking, non-government job holding, non-entity. Mom, suspicious of my activities, rarely entered my room when I was in it.

But there she was, looking down at me with a mixture of determination, distaste, and... pleading? Yes, that too.

"Wake up. Take your bath. Please SHAVE! And wear these FRESH clothes. No! Don't look for your jeans—I've put them all to wash. You are not going to look like these..." she pointed at the rock stars on my wall, "...this weekend."

"Why, Mom? Who's coming? And why should it affect me? I'll stick around in my room. Anyway, I'm meeting my friends later—I'll quietly slip off."

Mom seemed to gather courage. Her tone turned emotionally blackmail-y:
"The guests are coming to see you... and you must promise me you won't run away."

I sighed. It had to happen someday. I was of marriageable age and since I wasn't scoring with any women (long jaw, bushy eyebrows—thanks genes), Mom had decided to take matters into her own capable hands. It was matchmaking time.

I could've protested, been uncooperative, or just walked out. But my parents were such darlings. They'd never questioned me, even once—not when I fooled around, not when I sold ad space, not when I quit, not when I rejoined college, not even when I picked a job with an unpronounceable ad agency over a rock-solid Parsi firm or a software company. They quietly stood by. Whatever time I returned, warm food was on the table. Money was handed over without question the moment I ran out of my meagre salary.

I looked at her anxious face. I couldn't say no.

I nodded dumbly, like some prehistoric rock. That was enough for her. She shot off at Bolt-like speed, decorating the house and preparing a million things to present her son as a suitable prospect.

I buried myself in a book. Mom buried herself in her arrangements. Then they arrived. Mom ran around discussing the kind of car they'd come in. I sank deeper into my book. It was a pathetic novel where the hero got beaten up till the end, and his enemies were felled by dumb luck. Still, I gladly exchanged places with that loser.

The guests were the girl's parents. The father, a senior executive, got straight to business. He asked about my day, not casually—but in half-hour time slots.

"I've prepared a timetable for both my daughters," he said.

He proudly walked me through it. They woke up at 5 a.m., and every 30 minutes of their day was accounted for.

"From 9 to 9:45 PM, I allow them to fight," he said.

Images of WWE-style brawling danced in my head. Would I need to fight his daughter between 9:45 and 10:30 every night?

"No, no. Only verbal arguments," he clarified, as if reading my thoughts.

Then Dad and Mom started whispering frantically. They were staring at something. Dad slid a photo into my hands and whispered, "Look at this before you say anything that can be construed as a 'yes'..."

It was a studio photo of the girl. Not unusual for the time. But she looked like she was dressed for a Jayalalithaa biopic—giant garland, oil-slicked hair. More like a sacrificial goat than a bride-to-be. I felt trapped. Between a timetabled life and an oversized garland, my future was leaking away—like the oil from her hair.

Mom rescued me:

"Our son is too young and not ready for marriage for a few years..."

I breathed easy. But not for long.

One busy weekday, Mom called. "Meet us at Bharat Café, Ghatkopar, 7 p.m." Somehow, I handed off my work and rushed there. The café was packed. After some searching, I spotted Mom and Dad, squished into a seat with a beaming couple.

"She's waiting for you upstairs."

Before I could roll my eyes, the man explained, "My eldest daughter met my son-in-law here—lucky, you see!" Mom gave me a pleading look.

Upstairs, I found a girl. Just as I settled down, squawking broke out below. Her father was yelling, "Wrong girl!" Oops. The two of us located the correct girl.

I sat across from her. The waiters were grinning knowingly. I felt like part of an arranged marriage statistic. I focused on the menu.

She broke the silence, "Why do Western boys always think Central girls are downmarket?"

The conversation took off from there. She talked. I listened. She didn't cook, didn't intend to work, and her parents brought everything to her—right into her hands.

I just ate.

When I paid the bill, she looked surprised. "Wait, I've still more to tell—"

I apologized, mumbled about being tired, and left.

Mom was eager for a report.

"So, will you find living with her conducive?"

"Actually Mom, you should answer that—she said you'll

have to cook for her and serve her at the table. If that's cool with you and Dad, I'm cool."

There was no Bharat Café round 2.

The second-class compartment of the Geetanjali Express is a microcosm of India. From my top berth, I watched people fight for seats, then settle into camaraderie. Only Mom looked tense.

A distant relative had told her about a girl in Calcutta. It was too short notice for a proper photo, so we endured the train.

We arrived and met the girl's family for the chooda-barfi routine. Thirty people sat watching us silently. I suggested lunch the next day. The girl agreed, trance-like.

At the hotel, things fell into place when a group of hotel trainees burst in—she clearly knew them. One guy remained, just looking at her. She looked back.

I felt like Salman in Kuch Kuch Hota Hai. I quietly left.

I walked around Calcutta all afternoon. I couldn't return home right away—would've embarrassed her. I got back late, asked Mom to pack up. She never asked questions. I never offered answers.

I was thankful—for the girl's honesty. I'd rather endure 4 days on a train than a lifetime as a second-class option.

By now, Mom felt like she was the bad luck element in every match. So she pushed me out to meet girls alone.

All rejected me.

One, because I wasn't a karate expert (she was a classical dancer and wanted an equal).
One, because I confused Zen Buddhism with the Dalai Lama and mentioned Robert Pirsig. ("Not funny. Fail.")
Two, because I wasn't a banker.
One, because she earned more than me.

I was consistent. In failure.

And then—one Sunday—Mom woke me up. Again.
But this time, she wasn't forceful. She looked beaten. She blamed herself for all the rejections.

I joked, "Why do I need a wife, Mom, when you're here to fuss over me?"
It made her smile—for a while.

Then they arrived.

She wore a deep blue sari. As she removed her slippers quietly, I noticed something—calmness. Dignity. I offered her a chair. She smiled.

It felt... nice.

When we met privately, I asked if:

She had a checklist I had to match

She expected me to fight her every night

She had a philosophical issue with advertising

She wanted me to know the difference between Zen, Samurai, and Shogun

She worried about what Western boys thought about Central girls

She cared how much I earned

She'd prefer I was a banker

She just laughed.

And that's how it all began.

THE END

P.S.

My mom wouldn't believe me when I gave her the thumbs up sign soon after the meeting. She took me aside explained that she didn't wish to force me into marriage. Neither did I have to agree to the alliance, merely to keep her happy. She assured me that she would accept my 'no' and was willing to scout more.

Then, she gave me precisely one second to respond before rushing off to the telephone to confirm the engagement with my soon-to-be-wife's folks.